The Ultimate Project Management Handbook

Welcome to The Ultimate Project Management Handbook a comprehensive guide designed to help beginners, novices and experts understand the principles and practices of true project management. Whether you're a student, a professional starting your career, or an enthusiast looking to enhance your project management skills, this book will take you step-by-step through the fundamentals and best practices of managing successful projects.

Table of Contents

Chapter 1: What is Project Management

- Defining projects and project management
- The importance of project management in various industries
- Key project management concepts and terminology

Chapter 2: Initiating a Project

- Identifying project stakeholders
- Conducting a project needs assessment
- Defining project objectives, scope, and deliverables
- Creating a project charter

Chapter 3: Planning Your Project

- Developing a Project Plan
- Creating a work breakdown structure (WBS)
- Estimating project time and resources
- Allocating tasks and responsibilities
- Risk assessment and management planning

Chapter 4: Organizing Your Project Team

- Assembling the Project Team
- Understanding Roles & Responsibilities
- Improving Team Communication & Collaboration
- Resolving Conflicts within the team

Chapter 5: Executing the Project

- Implementing the project plan
- Monitoring project progress and performance
- Managing changes and unexpected issues
- Delivering on time and within budget

Chapter 6: Managing Project Risks

- Identifying potential risks
- Analyzing and prioritizing risks
- Creating risk response plans
- Continuous risk monitoring and mitigation

Chapter 7: Quality Control and Assurance

- Understanding quality in project deliverables
- Developing a quality management plan
- Conducting quality assurance and control activities
- Ensuring customer satisfaction

Chapter 8: Communication and Reporting

- Effective project communication strategies
- Creating progress reports
- Conducting project status meetings
- Managing project documentation

Chapter 9: Project Closure and Evaluation

- Closing out the project
- Conducting project reviews and evaluations
- Capturing lessons learned for future projects

Chapter 10: Project Management Tools and Software

- Introduction to project management tools
- Popular project management software
- Utilizing technology for efficient project management

Chapter 11: Agile Project Management

- Understanding Agile principles and methodologies
- Scrum, Kanban, and other Agile frameworks
- Implementing Agile practices in your projects

Chapter 12: Real-world Project Management Examples

- Case studies of successful project management
- Learning from project failures and challenges
- Adapting best practices for your projects

Chapter 1: What is Project Management

Project Management is the discipline of planning, organizing, and managing resources to achieve specific goals and objectives within a defined timeframe. It is a systematic approach to successfully completing projects and involves coordinating various tasks, activities, and people to deliver desired outcomes while adhering to constraints such as time, budget, and scope.

10 Key Critical Components of Project Management

1. **Project Scope:** Defining the specific goals, deliverables, and tasks required to complete the project successfully.
2. **Project Schedule:** Establishing a timeline for project activities, outlining the start and finish dates for each task.
3. **Resource Management:** Identifying and allocating the necessary resources, including human resources, equipment, and materials, to carry out the project.
4. **Risk Management:** Identifying potential risks and uncertainties that could impact the project and developing strategies to mitigate or respond to them.
5. **Cost Management:** Estimating and controlling the project budget to ensure that the project is completed within the allocated financial resources.
6. **Quality Management:** Ensuring that project deliverables meet the required standards and align with stakeholder expectations.
7. **Communication Management:** Establishing effective communication channels to keep stakeholders informed about the project's progress, changes, and challenges.
8. **Team Management:** Building and leading a cohesive project team, defining roles and responsibilities, and fostering collaboration.
9. **Change Management:** Handling changes to the project scope or requirements and assessing their impact on the project's objectives.
10. **Project Closure:** Completing all necessary activities to finalize the project, including delivering the final product, conducting project reviews, and documenting lessons learned.

Project Management can be applied to a wide range of industries and projects, from constructing buildings and developing software to organizing events and launching marketing campaigns. Various project management methodologies exist, such as the traditional Waterfall approach and the Agile methodology, each suited to different project types and requirements.

A successful project manager must possess strong organizational and leadership skills, excellent communication abilities, and the ability to adapt to changing circumstances. By effectively managing projects, organizations can increase efficiency, reduce risks, and ensure that projects are completed on time and within budget, leading to successful outcomes and satisfied stakeholders.

Defining A Project & Project Management

A project is a temporary and unique endeavor with a specific goal or objective, aimed at creating a product, service, or result. It is characterized by its distinct beginning and end, well-defined scope, and limited resources, such as time, budget, and personnel. Projects are undertaken to achieve something that hasn't been done before or to improve upon existing processes, products, or services. They are different from ongoing operations, which are repetitive and continuous in nature.

5 Key characteristics of projects include

1. **Temporary Nature:** Projects have a defined start and end date, with a clear initiation and closure phase.
2. **Unique Outcome:** Each project produces a unique deliverable or result, which could be a product, service, or solution.
3. **Specific Objectives:** Projects are undertaken to achieve specific goals or objectives, which are clearly defined during the project planning phase.
4. **Constraints:** Projects have limitations on resources such as time, budget, and team members, and the success of a project depends on effectively managing these constraints.
5. **Interdisciplinary:** Projects often require collaboration across different disciplines and departments to bring together diverse expertise.

Project management is the systematic application of knowledge, skills, tools, and techniques to plan, execute, monitor, and control projects from start to finish. It is a structured approach that ensures projects are completed efficiently, within budget, and meeting the intended objectives. Project management involves coordinating and balancing various elements of the project, such as scope, time, cost, quality, resources, risks, and stakeholder expectations.

5 Key aspects of Project Management include

1. **Initiation:** Defining the project's purpose, objectives, and scope. This includes identifying key stakeholders, understanding their needs, and assessing the feasibility of the project.
2. **Planning:** Creating a comprehensive project plan that outlines the tasks, activities, resources, and timelines required to achieve the project objectives. This phase involves defining the project's scope, schedule, budget, and risk management strategies.
3. **Execution:** Implementing the project plan by coordinating and directing resources, managing the team, and executing the defined tasks and activities.
4. **Monitoring and Control:** Regularly tracking project progress, comparing it to the planned schedule and budget, and making necessary adjustments to ensure the project stays on track.
5. **Closure:** Formalizing the completion of the project, delivering the final product or service, conducting project reviews, and documenting lessons learned for future projects.

Effective project management ensures that projects are delivered successfully, meeting the expectations of stakeholders and aligning with the organization's strategic objectives. Project managers play a crucial role in overseeing the project's execution, communicating with stakeholders, managing risks, resolving conflicts, and ensuring the project's ultimate success.

The Importance of Project Management Across Industries

Project management plays a vital role in various industries, contributing to the successful execution of projects and overall organizational success. Below are some of the most critical key reasons why project management is essential across industries:

- **Optimized Resource Utilization:** Project management ensures efficient use of resources, including time, money, materials, and human resources. It helps prevent wastage and ensures that resources are allocated where they are most needed.
- **Clear Objectives and Scope:** Project management defines clear project objectives and scope, helping to avoid scope creep and ensuring that the project team focuses on delivering the desired outcomes.
- **Risk Mitigation:** Identifying and managing risks is a fundamental aspect of project management. By proactively addressing potential risks, industries can minimize disruptions and prevent costly failures.
- **Improved Time Management:** Projects often have specific timelines, and effective project management enables industries to meet deadlines and deliver projects on time, leading to increased efficiency and customer satisfaction.
- **Quality Assurance:** Project management emphasizes quality control and assurance throughout the project lifecycle. By adhering to quality standards, industries can deliver products or services that meet or exceed customer expectations.
- **Enhanced Communication:** Proper project management fosters transparent and efficient communication among team members, stakeholders, and clients. This reduces misunderstandings and ensures that everyone is on the same page.
- **Increased Flexibility and Adaptability:** Project management methodologies, such as Agile, enable industries to adapt to changing requirements and customer feedback, allowing for more responsive and customer-centric solutions.
- **Customer Satisfaction:** Delivering projects successfully within scope, budget, and timeline satisfies customers and builds trust, leading to improved customer loyalty and positive word-of-mouth referrals.
- **Innovation and Continuous Improvement:** Project management encourages industries to embrace innovation and continuous improvement. Through project lessons learned, organizations can refine their processes and approaches for future projects.
- **Efficient Decision Making:** Project management provides a structured approach to decision-making, helping industries make informed choices based on data and analysis.
- **Regulatory Compliance:** In industries with strict regulatory requirements, project management ensures that projects adhere to relevant laws and regulations.
- **Competitive Advantage:** Industries that excel in project management gain a competitive edge by delivering projects faster, with higher quality and lower costs, positioning them as market leaders.

Industries ranging from construction and engineering to information technology, healthcare, marketing, and finance benefit from implementing robust project management practices. Regardless of the sector, project management is a valuable discipline that enables industries to achieve their objectives, drive innovation, and adapt to a rapidly changing business landscape.

Key Project Management Concepts and Terminology

Understanding key project management concepts and terminology is crucial for effectively managing projects. Here are some essential concepts and terms commonly used in project management:

- **Project:** A temporary endeavor with a specific start and end date, aimed at creating a unique product, service, or result.
- **Project Scope:** The detailed description of the project's objectives, deliverables, tasks, and boundaries, defining what will and will not be included in the project.
- **Work Breakdown Structure (WBS):** A hierarchical representation of the project's deliverables and work packages, breaking down the project into manageable tasks.
- **Project Charter:** A formal document that authorizes the project, defines its objectives, and identifies key stakeholders and their roles.
- **Project Management Plan (PMP):** A comprehensive document that outlines how the project will be executed, monitored, controlled, and closed.
- **Stakeholders:** Individuals or groups with an interest in the project's outcome or who can impact the project's success.
- **Milestone:** A significant point or event in a project, often marking the completion of a major deliverable or the achievement of a critical objective.
- **Critical Path:** The sequence of tasks that determine the shortest duration for completing the project, and any delay in these tasks will affect the project's overall timeline.
- **Gantt Chart:** A visual representation of the project schedule, displaying tasks as bars along a timeline.
- **Resource Allocation:** The process of assigning and managing resources, such as personnel, equipment, and materials, to the project tasks.
- **Risk Management:** The process of identifying, assessing, and responding to potential risks that could impact the project's success.
- **Issue Management:** The process of identifying and addressing problems or challenges that arise during the project.
- **Change Management:** The process of managing changes to the project scope, schedule, or budget and ensuring that changes are properly evaluated and approved.
- **Quality Assurance (QA) and Quality Control (QC):** QA involves processes to ensure that the project's deliverables meet the required quality standards, while QC involves inspecting the deliverables to identify defects or issues.
- **Communication Plan:** A plan outlining how project information will be communicated to stakeholders, ensuring effective and timely communication.
- **Project Baseline:** The approved version of the project scope, schedule, and budget, against which actual performance is measured.
- **Project Closure:** The formal process of ending the project, including delivering the final product or service, conducting project reviews, and documenting lessons learned.
- **Agile Project Management:** An iterative and incremental approach to project management, emphasizing flexibility and customer collaboration.
- **Project Portfolio Management (PPM):** The centralized management of multiple projects to ensure they align with the organization's strategic goals and maximize overall success.
- **Lessons Learned:** Insights gained from project experiences, documenting successes and failures for future project improvements.

These concepts and terms form the foundation of project management knowledge and practice. Understanding them helps project managers and teams effectively plan, execute, and control projects, leading to successful project outcomes.

Chapter 2: Initiating a Project

Initiating a project is the critical first step in the project management process. In this chapter, we will explore the essential elements of project initiation, including defining project objectives, identifying stakeholders, conducting a needs assessment, and creating a project charter. By mastering the art of project initiation, you set the stage for a successful project execution.

Defining Project Objectives

- Understanding the importance of clear project objectives
- Techniques for defining SMART (Specific, Measurable, Achievable, Relevant, Time-bound) project objectives
- Aligning project objectives with organizational goals and strategic vision

Identifying Stakeholders

- Recognizing key stakeholders and their roles in the project
- Stakeholder analysis: assessing interests, influence, and level of involvement
- Strategies for managing stakeholder expectations and engagement throughout the project

Conducting a Needs Assessment

- Techniques for conducting a thorough needs assessment to understand project requirements
- Identifying project constraints and limitations
- Analyzing potential risks and opportunities in the project initiation phase

Creating a Project Charter

- Defining the purpose and components of a project charter
- Developing a project scope statement within the charter
- Including key elements such as project objectives, deliverables, milestones, and resources
- Gaining approval and buy-in from stakeholders for the project charter

Developing a Preliminary Project Schedule

- Outlining the major phases and activities required for the project
- Estimating the time required for each activity and creating a preliminary project schedule
- Understanding the critical path and its significance in the project timeline

Allocating Initial Resources

- Identifying and allocating the necessary resources for the project initiation phase
- Assessing resource availability and constraints

- Developing contingency plans for resource shortages or changes

Risk Identification and Initial Mitigation

1. Identifying potential risks during the project initiation stage
2. Conducting a SWOT (Strengths, Weaknesses, Opportunities, Threats) analysis
3. Outlining initial risk mitigation strategies and plans

Getting Stakeholder Approval

- Presenting the project charter and preliminary project schedule to stakeholders
- Addressing questions and concerns raised by stakeholders
- Obtaining formal approval and commitment for the project to proceed

By completing the project initiation phase, you have laid the foundation for a successful project journey. Initiating a project effectively sets the stage for clear objectives, stakeholder alignment, and a well-defined scope. As you move forward with the project, remember to keep communication lines open, manage risks diligently, and adapt to any changes that may arise. The next chapter will guide you through the essential steps of project planning and preparing for the project's execution phase.

Identifying Project Stakeholders

Identifying project stakeholders is a crucial step in project management as it helps ensure that all relevant individuals or groups with an interest in the project are identified and involved appropriately. Stakeholders can significantly impact the project's success and engaging them early on can lead to better project outcomes and increased support. Here are the 10 key steps to identify project stakeholders:

1. **Brainstorming:** Start by brainstorming with your project team to identify potential stakeholders. Consider anyone who may be affected by the project, has an interest in its outcome, or has the authority to influence its success.
2. **Consult Project Documentation:** Review any relevant project documentation, such as the project proposal or requirements, to identify stakeholders mentioned or implied.
3. **Internal Stakeholders:** Identify stakeholders within your organization, such as senior management, department heads, project team members, and employees who may be impacted by the project.
4. **External Stakeholders:** Look beyond the organization to identify external stakeholders. This may include customers, suppliers, regulatory authorities, local communities, shareholders, and any other parties affected by the project's outcomes.
5. **Interviews and Surveys:** Conduct interviews or surveys with key individuals or groups to gather their perspectives on the project and identify potential stakeholders.
6. **Stakeholder Categories:** Categorize stakeholders based on their level of influence and interest in the project. Common categories include primary (directly impacted), secondary (indirectly impacted), positive (supportive), negative (opposed), and neutral stakeholders.
7. **Stakeholder Analysis:** Analyze each stakeholder's interests, needs, concerns, and potential impact on the project. Understand their expectations and how they align with the project objectives.
8. **Mapping Stakeholders:** Create a stakeholder map or matrix that visually represents the relationships between stakeholders and their level of influence or interest in the project.
9. **Validation and Verification:** Verify the identified stakeholders with other team members, project sponsors, or subject matter experts to ensure comprehensive coverage.
10. **Ongoing Review:** Stakeholder identification should be an ongoing process throughout the project's lifecycle. New stakeholders may emerge, and existing stakeholders' interests may change over time.

Remember that effective stakeholder management involves engaging and communicating with stakeholders throughout the project, addressing their concerns, and keeping them informed about project progress. By understanding and involving stakeholders, project managers can build strong relationships, gain support, and navigate potential challenges more effectively.

Conducting a Project Needs Assessment

Conducting a project needs assessment is a critical step in the project initiation phase. It involves gathering information to understand the current situation, identify project requirements, and determine whether the project aligns with organizational goals. Below is a step-by-step guide on how to conduct a project needs assessment and the 12 key steps:

1. **Define the Purpose and Scope of the Assessment:** Clearly outline the objectives of the needs assessment and the specific aspects of the project you intend to assess. Define the scope of the assessment to avoid unnecessary data collection.
2. **Identify Key Stakeholders:** Determine the individuals or groups who can provide valuable insights for the needs assessment. This may include project sponsors, end-users, subject matter experts, customers, and other relevant parties.
3. **Gather Background Information:** Collect existing data, reports, and documentation related to the project or the problem it aims to solve. This can include previous project reports, market research, customer feedback, and internal documents.
4. **Conduct Interviews and Focus Groups:** Schedule interviews or focus group sessions with key stakeholders to gather their perspectives and insights. Ask open-ended questions to encourage discussion and explore their needs, expectations, and concerns related to the project.
5. **Distribute Surveys:** Prepare and distribute surveys to a broader group of stakeholders to collect quantitative data and opinions on specific aspects of the project. Surveys can help gather data from a larger sample size efficiently.
6. **Perform Site Visits or Observations:** If applicable, conduct site visits or observations to gain firsthand knowledge of the project environment, processes, and challenges.
7. **Analyze Data and Identify Trends:** Review and analyze the data collected from interviews, focus groups, and surveys. Look for patterns, trends, and common themes to understand the most significant needs and priorities.
8. **Prioritize Needs:** Based on the analysis, prioritize the identified needs based on their impact on the project's success and the organization's objectives. Determine which needs are critical and must be addressed during project planning and execution.
9. **Validate Findings:** Share the needs assessment findings with stakeholders to ensure accuracy and completeness. Seek feedback and validation to confirm that the identified needs align with their expectations.
10. **Document the Needs Assessment Report:** Prepare a comprehensive report summarizing the findings of the needs assessment. Include a clear overview of the identified needs, the data collected, the analysis performed, and the prioritization of needs.
11. **Present the Findings:** Present the needs assessment report to project sponsors, key stakeholders, and the project team. Clearly communicate the implications of the findings and how they will influence the project's direction.
12. **Incorporate Findings in Project Planning:** Use the needs assessment results to inform the project's goals, objectives, scope, and strategies during the planning phase. Ensure that the project plan addresses the identified needs effectively.

By conducting a thorough needs assessment, project managers can gain valuable insights, establish a strong foundation for the project, and increase the chances of delivering a successful solution that meets stakeholders' expectations.

Defining Project Objectives, Scope & Deliverables

Defining project objectives, scope, and deliverables is a crucial step in project management. These elements provide clarity and direction, ensuring that everyone involved in the project understands what needs to be achieved and what is expected. Here's how to define each of these components:

- **Project Objectives:** Project objectives are the specific, measurable goals that the project aims to achieve. They define the desired outcomes and the purpose of the project. When defining project objectives, consider the SMART criteria:
  - Specific: Objectives should be well-defined and clear, leaving no room for ambiguity.
  - Measurable: Objectives should be quantifiable so that progress can be measured and evaluated.
  - Achievable: Objectives should be realistic and feasible given the available resources and constraints.
  - Relevant: Objectives should align with the organization's strategic goals and contribute to its overall success.
  - Time-bound: Objectives should have a specific timeframe or deadline for completion.

For example, a project objective for a software development project could be "To develop and launch a user-friendly mobile app for our customers within six months, increasing customer engagement by 20%."

- **Project Scope:** Project scope defines the boundaries of the project, outlining what will and will not be included. It sets the limits and provides a clear understanding of the work to be done. Scope is critical for preventing scope creep, which can lead to increased costs and project delays.
  - Inclusions: Clearly define the features, functionalities, and tasks that the project will deliver.
  - Exclusions: Specify what will not be part of the project to manage stakeholders' expectations.
  - Assumptions: Outline any assumptions made during scoping to set expectations on uncertainties.

For example, the scope for a website development project could include building a homepage, product pages, and a checkout process while excluding additional language translations that will be considered in a future project phase.

- **Project Deliverables:** Project deliverables are the tangible results or outputs of the project. They are the specific items, products, or services that the project will produce and deliver to stakeholders upon completion. Defining deliverables is essential for measuring project success and ensuring that the project meets its objectives.
  - Specificity: Deliverables should be well-defined, leaving no room for ambiguity.
  - Verifiability: Deliverables should be measurable and verifiable to determine if they have been achieved.
  - Completeness: Ensure that all key deliverables necessary for project success are identified.

For example, the deliverables for a marketing campaign project could include a social media strategy document, a series of promotional videos, and a post-campaign performance report.

By clearly defining project objectives, scope, and deliverables, project managers can set a clear direction, manage stakeholders' expectations, and ensure that the project remains focused on achieving its intended outcomes. It also serves as a reference point throughout the project to track progress and make informed decisions.

Creating a Project Charter

Creating a project charter is a crucial step in project management as it formally authorizes the project and provides a clear, concise overview of its objectives, scope, and key stakeholders. The project charter serves as a foundational document that guides the project throughout its lifecycle. Here's a step-by-step guide on how to create a Project Charter:

- **Title and Project Overview:** Begin the project charter with a clear and descriptive title that represents the project. Provide an overview of the project, summarizing its purpose, objectives, and key deliverables.
- **Project Objectives and Success Criteria:** Clearly state the specific, measurable objectives that the project aims to achieve. Define the success criteria or key performance indicators (KPIs) that will be used to measure the project's success.
- **Project Scope:** Outline the project's boundaries by describing what will be included and what will be excluded. Clearly define the scope of work to prevent scope creep and ensure alignment with stakeholders' expectations.
- **Key Stakeholders and Roles:** Identify the main stakeholders involved in the project, including project sponsors, team members, and other important parties. Clearly define their roles and responsibilities in the project.
- **High-Level Timeline:** Provide a high-level timeline for the project, indicating the start and end dates, major milestones, and key project phases.
- **Budget and Resources:** Include an estimate of the project budget and the resources required for successful project execution. This could include personnel, equipment, materials, and any external support.
- **Project Risks and Assumptions:** Identify potential risks that could impact the project and briefly outline initial risk mitigation strategies. Also, list any assumptions made during the project charter development.
- **Approvals and Signatures:** Include a section for project stakeholders to provide formal approval of the project charter. This section should include space for signatures from key stakeholders, indicating their commitment to the project.
- **Project Manager and Authority:** Specify the project manager's name and their level of authority in decision-making and project execution.
- **Review and Update Process:** Outline the process for reviewing and updating the project charter as the project progresses. This ensures that the document remains relevant and accurate throughout the project lifecycle.
- **Communication Plan:** Briefly describe the communication approach for the project, including how project updates will be communicated to stakeholders and how feedback will be collected.
- **Additional Information:** Include any other relevant information, specific to the project's context, that provides a comprehensive understanding of the project's purpose and objectives.

Remember that the Project Charter should be a concise document that provides a clear overview of the project and gains formal approval from key stakeholders. It acts as a reference point for decision-making, scope control, and project management throughout the project's lifecycle. Regularly revisit and update the Project Charter as needed to reflect changes and keep stakeholders informed.

Chapter 3: Planning Your Project

In this chapter, we dive into the essential process of planning your project. Effective project planning is the backbone of successful project management as it lays the groundwork for executing the project efficiently, minimizing risks, and achieving project objectives. Let's explore the key steps and considerations involved in planning your project.

Defining Project Scope and Objectives

- Reviewing the project charter to confirm project objectives and scope
- Refining project objectives to ensure they are specific, measurable, achievable, relevant, and time-bound (SMART)
- Defining the scope of work and deliverables to be produced during the project

Work Breakdown Structure (WBS)

- Creating a detailed Work Breakdown Structure (WBS) to break the project into manageable tasks and sub-tasks
- Organizing the WBS into hierarchical levels for better project understanding and management
- Assigning responsibility for each task to the project team members

Project Schedule and Timeline

- Developing a comprehensive project schedule that includes task durations, dependencies, and milestones
- Utilizing tools like Gantt charts to visualize the project timeline and critical path
- Establishing a realistic project timeline to manage expectations and deadlines

Resource Management

- Identifying the resources required for each task, including human resources, equipment, and materials
- Allocating resources efficiently to optimize project performance and minimize delays
- Addressing potential resource constraints and developing contingency plans

Risk Management and Mitigation

- Identifying potential risks and uncertainties that could impact the project
- Analyzing the probability and impact of each risk to prioritize mitigation efforts
- Developing risk response strategies to avoid or minimize potential negative impacts

Quality Assurance and Control

- Defining quality standards and expectations for project deliverables
- Implementing quality control measures throughout the project to ensure compliance
- Conducting regular audits and inspections to maintain high-quality outcomes

Communication and Stakeholder Management

- Creating a communication plan to ensure effective information flow among project team members and stakeholders
- Addressing stakeholder needs and concerns through regular updates and engagement
- Managing stakeholder expectations and proactively addressing potential issues

Budgeting and Cost Management

- Preparing a detailed project budget that accounts for all costs, including labor, materials, equipment, and contingencies
- Monitoring and controlling project expenses to stay within budget constraints
- Addressing cost overruns and variations with appropriate corrective actions

Developing a Project Plan

Developing a comprehensive project plan is a critical step in project management. A well-structured project plan provides a roadmap for executing the project, defines tasks and responsibilities, and helps manage resources, time, and risks effectively. Here's a step-by-step guide to developing a project plan:

- **Project Objectives and Scope:** Begin by revisiting the project objectives and scope defined earlier. Ensure that they are clear, specific, and aligned with organizational goals.
- **Work Breakdown Structure (WBS):** Create a detailed Work Breakdown Structure (WBS) that breaks down the project into smaller, manageable tasks. Organize tasks into hierarchical levels, with the top level representing major project phases and subsequent levels breaking tasks into sub-tasks.
- **Task Duration and Dependencies:** Estimate the duration for each task based on historical data or expert judgment. Identify task dependencies to understand which tasks must be completed before others can start.
- **Task Assignments and Resources:** Assign responsibilities for each task to specific team members based on their skills and expertise. Ensure that resources, including human resources, equipment, and materials, are allocated appropriately to each task.
- **Project Schedule:** Using the task durations and dependencies, create a detailed project schedule. Utilize project management tools such as Gantt charts or project scheduling software to visualize the timeline and critical path.
- **Risk Assessment and Mitigation:** Identify potential risks that may affect the project's success. Assess their probability and impact and develop strategies to mitigate or manage these risks throughout the project lifecycle.
- **Quality Management:** Define quality standards and expectations for project deliverables. Plan quality control activities to ensure that deliverables meet these standards.
- **Communication Plan:** Develop a communication plan that outlines how project information will be communicated to team members, stakeholders, and other relevant parties. Define communication channels, frequency, and recipients.
- **Budget and Cost Management:** Prepare a detailed project budget, considering all costs, including labor, materials, equipment, and contingency funds. Monitor and control project expenses to stay within budget constraints.

- **Stakeholder Engagement:** Plan for stakeholder engagement and management throughout the project. Understand stakeholders' needs, concerns, and expectations and develop strategies to address them.
- **Change Management:** Outline procedures for managing changes to the project scope, schedule, or budget. Establish a change control process to evaluate and approve changes effectively.
- **Project Documentation:** Create a comprehensive project documentation repository to keep all project-related documents, reports, and records organized and accessible.
- **Review and Approval:** Review the project plan with key stakeholders, project sponsors, and team members to gather feedback and obtain formal approval before proceeding.
- **Project Kick-Off:** Conduct a project kick-off meeting to communicate the project plan, objectives, scope, and roles to all team members and stakeholders.

Remember that the project plan is a dynamic document that may evolve throughout the project. Regularly monitor and update the plan as needed to reflect changes, progress, and new information. A well-developed project plan serves as a valuable guide, ensuring that the project stays on track, manages risks effectively, and delivers successful outcomes.

Creating A Work Breakdown Structure (WBS)

Creating a Work Breakdown Structure (WBS) is a systematic approach to breaking down a complex project into smaller, manageable tasks. The WBS provides a visual representation of the project's hierarchical structure, helping project managers and team members understand the project's scope and deliverables. Here's a step-by-step guide to creating a WBS:

- **Identify Major Deliverables:** Start by listing the major deliverables or outcomes that the project is expected to produce. These are the high-level components of the project.
- **Divide Deliverables into Sub-Deliverables:** Break down each major deliverable into smaller, more manageable sub-deliverables. Each sub-deliverable represents a distinct component of the major deliverable.
- **Keep Breaking Down Tasks:** Continue breaking down the sub-deliverables into smaller tasks until each task is specific and manageable. The goal is to create a clear and well-structured hierarchy of tasks.
- **Use Verb-Noun Format:** Use a consistent naming convention for tasks in the WBS. A common practice is to use a verb-noun format, where the verb represents the action and the noun describes the object of the action. For example, "Develop Marketing Strategy" or "Test Software Functionality."
- **Maintain Logical Sequence:** Arrange the tasks in a logical sequence to represent the order in which they need to be completed. Dependencies between tasks should be evident in the WBS.
- **Assign WBS Codes:** Assign unique codes to each element in the WBS to aid in organizing and referencing the tasks. The codes can be numeric or alphanumeric.
- **Review and Validate:** Review the WBS with the project team and key stakeholders to ensure that all necessary tasks are included and that there are no gaps or duplications.
- **Use WBS Software or Tools:** Consider using project management software or specialized WBS tools to create and manage the WBS efficiently. These tools often offer features like drag-and-drop functionality and automatic code generation.
- **Update as Needed:** The WBS is not a static document. It may evolve as the project progresses, so be prepared to update and refine the WBS as needed.

Example of a Simple WBS for a Marketing Campaign:

Marketing Campaign

1.1 Develop Marketing Strategy
   1.1.1 Market Research
   1.1.2 Define Target Audience
   1.1.3 Set Campaign Goals
1.2 Design Marketing Materials
   1.2.1 Create Graphics and Artwork
   1.2.2 Write Copy and Content
   1.2.3 Design Landing Pages
1.3 Execute Marketing Campaign
   1.3.1 Social Media Promotion
   1.3.2 Email Marketing
   1.3.3 Content Publishing
1.4 Measure and Analyze Results
   1.4.1 Track Website Traffic
   1.4.2 Monitor Conversion Rates
   1.4.3 Analyze ROI and KPIs

The WBS provides a clear overview of the project's tasks and facilitates better project planning, scheduling, and resource allocation. It serves as a foundation for project execution and helps maintain focus on the project's objectives.

Estimating Project Time & Resources

Estimating project time and resources is a critical aspect of project planning as it helps determine the project schedule and resource requirements. Accurate estimations are essential for successful project execution and meeting stakeholder expectations. Here's a step-by-step guide on how to estimate project time and resources:

- **Define Project Scope and Objectives:** Have a clear understanding of the project scope and objectives before estimating time and resources. A well-defined scope ensures that you know what needs to be accomplished.
- **Break Down the Work:** Use the Work Breakdown Structure (WBS) created earlier to break down the project into smaller, manageable tasks. Each task should be specific and have a clear outcome.
- **Identify Task Dependencies:** Determine the relationships between tasks to understand which tasks are dependent on others. This helps ensure a logical sequence of tasks in the project schedule.
- **Estimate Task Duration:** Work with the project team to estimate the time required to complete each task. Consider historical data, expert judgment, and any other relevant information to arrive at realistic estimates.
- **Consider Resource Availability:** Assess the availability of resources, including personnel, equipment, and materials. Take into account any constraints or limitations that could affect resource allocation.
- **Account for Contingencies:** Include contingency time and resources in the estimates to accommodate unexpected delays or changes in the project.
- **Use Estimation Techniques:** Utilize various estimation techniques such as Analogous Estimating (using historical data from similar projects), Parametric Estimating (using mathematical models), and Three-Point Estimating (using optimistic, pessimistic, and most likely estimates) to improve accuracy.
- **Create the Project Schedule:** Based on the estimated task durations and dependencies, develop a project schedule using project management tools like Gantt charts or project scheduling software.
- **Resource Allocation:** Assign resources to each task based on their availability and skillset. Ensure that resources are allocated efficiently to avoid overloading or underutilization.

- **Validate Estimates:** Review the time and resource estimates with the project team and key stakeholders to validate their accuracy and obtain feedback.
- **Update and Refine:** Project time and resource estimates may change as the project progresses or when new information becomes available. Be prepared to update and refine the estimates as needed.
- **Monitor and Control:** Throughout the project, monitor actual progress against the estimated time and resource usage. Use this information to make necessary adjustments and control the project's performance.

Remember that time and resource estimation is an iterative process, and it requires collaboration among project team members and stakeholders. Continuous improvement in estimation accuracy will lead to more successful project planning and execution.

Allocating Tasks & Responsibilities

Allocating tasks and responsibilities is a crucial part of project planning and execution. Proper task allocation ensures that each team member knows their role, responsibilities, and what is expected from them throughout the project. Here's a step-by-step guide on how to allocate tasks and responsibilities effectively:

- **Review the Work Breakdown Structure (WBS):** Refer to the WBS created earlier to identify all the tasks and sub-tasks that need to be completed for the project. Each task should be clearly defined and have a specific deliverable or outcome.
- **Identify Skillsets and Competencies:** Understand the strengths, skills, and competencies of each team member. Consider their expertise and experience when assigning tasks.
- **Consider Workload and Availability:** Assess the workload and availability of each team member. Avoid overloading individuals with too many tasks or assigning tasks to team members who may already be fully occupied.
- **Match Tasks with Skills:** Match tasks with the appropriate team members who have the necessary skills and expertise to perform them effectively. Consider team members' interests and development opportunities as well.
- **Define Clear Responsibilities:** Clearly define the responsibilities of each team member for the tasks they are assigned. Ensure that everyone understands what is expected from them and the level of autonomy they have.
- **Set Deadlines:** Assign realistic deadlines for each task. Consider task dependencies, resource availability, and the project timeline when setting deadlines.
- **Communicate Expectations:** Communicate task assignments and responsibilities to each team member in a clear and concise manner. Make sure they understand their role and the importance of their contribution to the project's success.
- **Encourage Collaboration:** Promote collaboration among team members. Encourage them to communicate and support each other throughout the project.
- **Provide Resources and Support:** Ensure that team members have access to the necessary resources, tools, and information required to complete their tasks. Offer support and guidance whenever needed.
- **Monitor Progress:** Regularly monitor the progress of tasks and check whether team members are on track to meet deadlines. Address any issues or roadblocks promptly.
- **Adjust as Needed:** Be flexible in task allocation. If circumstances change or unexpected challenges arise, be ready to reassign tasks or adjust responsibilities accordingly.
- **Acknowledge Achievements:** Recognize and acknowledge the efforts and achievements of team members. Positive reinforcement boosts motivation and fosters a positive team environment.

By allocating tasks and responsibilities effectively, you create a well-coordinated and productive project team. Clarity in roles and expectations enhances collaboration and contributes to the successful completion of the project's objectives. Regularly communicate and maintain open lines of communication with the team to ensure that everyone remains informed and engaged throughout the project lifecycle.

Risk Assessment & Management Planning

Risk assessment and management planning are essential processes in project management that help identify potential risks, analyze their potential impact, and develop strategies to mitigate or address them. Effectively managing risks can significantly increase the chances of project success and minimize the negative impact of unforeseen events. Here's a step-by-step guide to risk assessment and management planning:

- **Identify Risks:** Gather the project team and stakeholders to identify potential risks that could impact the project. Brainstorming sessions, interviews, and historical data analysis can help identify a wide range of risks.
- **Categorize Risks:** Categorize risks into different types, such as technical, external, organizational, schedule-related, or budget-related. This helps in better understanding and managing risks effectively.
- **Risk Analysis:** Assess the probability and impact of each identified risk. Probability is the likelihood of the risk occurring, while impact is the extent of its effect on the project if it does occur. Prioritize risks based on their significance.
- **Risk Response Strategies:** Develop risk response strategies for each identified risk. There are four main strategies:
    1. Avoidance: Take actions to eliminate the risk or prevent it from occurring.
    2. Mitigation: Implement measures to reduce the likelihood or impact of the risk.
    3. Transfer: Shift the risk to another party, such as through insurance or outsourcing.
    4. Acceptance: Acknowledge that the risk may occur and have a contingency plan to deal with its consequences if it happens.

- **Develop a Risk Management Plan:** Create a comprehensive risk management plan that outlines how risks will be identified, analyzed, and managed throughout the project lifecycle. The plan should define roles and responsibilities, communication protocols, and escalation procedures.
- **Implement Risk Responses:** Actively implement the risk response strategies as defined in the risk management plan. This may involve allocating resources, updating project plans, or creating contingency plans.
- **Monitor and Review Risks:** Regularly monitor the identified risks and evaluate the effectiveness of the risk response strategies. Update the risk management plan as needed and adapt to changing circumstances.
- **Contingency Planning:** Develop contingency plans for high-impact risks that cannot be entirely avoided or mitigated. Contingency plans outline the actions to be taken if specific risks occur, allowing for a quick response to minimize the negative impact.
- **Communicate Risk Information:** Ensure effective communication of risk information to all relevant stakeholders, including project team members, sponsors, and customers. Transparent communication builds trust and support.
- **Lessons Learned:** After the project is completed, conduct a lesson's learned session to identify any new risks that emerged during the project and assess the effectiveness of risk management strategies. Use this information to improve risk management practices for future projects.

By proactively assessing and managing risks, project managers can navigate uncertainties more effectively, make informed decisions, and increase the likelihood of delivering a successful project within the defined constraints.

By diligently defining objectives, scoping the project, creating a detailed WBS, and developing a comprehensive schedule, you have set the project on the path to success. Remember, effective planning is an ongoing process, and as the project progresses, be ready to adapt and make necessary adjustments to ensure project success. In the next chapter, we will delve into executing your project, bringing your well-crafted plans to life.

Chapter 4: Organizing Your Project Team

In this chapter, we explore the crucial process of organizing your project team. A well-structured and cohesive team plays a significant role in the success of any project. We'll discuss the key steps involved in assembling the right team, defining roles and responsibilities, fostering collaboration, and ensuring effective team management.

Identifying Team Roles and Skillsets

- Assessing project requirements to identify the specific roles needed for the project.
- Defining the essential skills and expertise required for each role.
- Determining the optimal team size to achieve project objectives efficiently.

Recruiting and Onboarding Team Members

- Developing a recruitment plan to attract suitable candidates for the project.
- Conducting interviews and assessments to select the most qualified team members.
- Creating an effective onboarding process to integrate new team members smoothly.

Team Communication and Collaboration

- Establishing clear communication channels to ensure efficient information flow.
- Implementing collaboration tools and practices to encourage teamwork and knowledge sharing.
- Fostering a positive team culture that promotes open communication and respect.

Setting Expectations and Goals

- Defining individual and team goals that align with the project's objectives.
- Ensuring team members understand their roles, responsibilities, and performance expectations.
- Encouraging accountability and ownership of tasks.

Building a High-Performing Team

- Recognizing and leveraging individual strengths and diversity within the team.
- Providing opportunities for professional growth and development.
- Facilitating team-building activities to strengthen relationships and trust.

Conflict Resolution and Problem-Solving

- Developing conflict resolution strategies to address any issues that may arise.
- Encouraging open discussions and constructive feedback to resolve conflicts.
- Implementing problem-solving techniques to overcome challenges and roadblocks.

Team Motivation and Engagement

- Implementing motivational strategies to keep team members engaged and committed.
- Recognizing and celebrating team achievements to boost morale.
- Addressing potential sources of demotivation and proactively mitigating them.

Team Performance Evaluation

- Implementing performance evaluation processes to assess individual and team progress.
- Providing constructive feedback and coaching to support continuous improvement.
- Recognizing outstanding contributions and areas for improvement.

Assembling the Project Team

Assembling the project team is a critical step in project management, as the success of the project largely depends on having the right people with the necessary skills and expertise. Here's a step-by-step guide on how to assemble the project team effectively:

- **Identify Project Roles and Responsibilities:** Based on the project scope and objectives, identify the specific roles needed for the project. Common project roles include project manager, team lead, subject matter experts, analysts, designers, developers, testers, and other relevant positions. Clearly define the responsibilities and expectations for each role.
- **Assess Skill Requirements:** Determine the skills and expertise required for each role. Consider technical skills, domain knowledge, project management capabilities, communication skills, and any other relevant qualifications.
- **Evaluate Existing Resources:** Assess the skills and availability of existing resources within the organization. Identify potential team members who have the required expertise and could be a good fit for the project.
- **Consider External Resources:** If additional skills are needed that are not available internally, consider recruiting external resources such as contractors, consultants, or freelancers. Clearly define their roles and scope of work.
- **Recruitment and Selection:** Conduct a thorough recruitment process to identify the best candidates for each role. Use interviews, assessments, and reference checks to evaluate candidates' qualifications, experience, and fit for the project.
- **Form the Project Team:** Once the appropriate candidates have been selected, assemble the project team. Announce team members' roles and responsibilities to create clarity and a sense of ownership.
- **Onboarding and Orientation:** Provide a comprehensive onboarding process for new team members. Familiarize them with the project, its objectives, the team's dynamics, and the organizational culture. This helps them integrate smoothly into the team and project environment.
- **Establish Communication Channels:** Set up effective communication channels for the project team to ensure smooth information flow. Use tools like project management software, messaging platforms, and regular team meetings to facilitate communication.
- **Encourage Collaboration and Teamwork:** Promote a collaborative and supportive team culture. Encourage team members to share ideas, work together, and leverage each other's strengths to achieve project goals.
- **Define Team Norms and Expectations:** Establish team norms and guidelines for collaboration, decision-making, conflict resolution, and meeting expectations. This fosters a positive team environment and helps prevent misunderstandings.
- **Continuous Training and Development:** Provide ongoing training and professional development opportunities for the team to enhance their skills and keep up with industry best practices.
- **Empower and Support the Team:** Empower the team to make decisions and take ownership of their tasks. Provide the necessary support, resources, and guidance to ensure their success.

By assembling the right project team and fostering a collaborative and supportive environment, you lay the foundation for a successful project execution. Regularly assess team dynamics, address any challenges, and ensure that the team remains motivated and engaged throughout the project's lifecycle.

Understanding Roles & Responsibilities

Understanding roles and responsibilities is essential for effective project management and successful project execution. Each team member should have a clear understanding of their role, what is expected from them, and how their contributions align with the project's objectives. Here's how to establish and communicate roles and responsibilities in a project:

- **Role Definition:** Identify and define the specific roles needed for the project. Common roles include project manager, team lead, subject matter experts, specialists, coordinators, and stakeholders. Clearly outline the responsibilities and authority associated with each role.
- **Role Alignment:** Ensure that each team member's role is aligned with their skills, expertise, and areas of specialization. Matching team members with suitable roles maximizes productivity and efficiency.
- **Roles in the Project Team:** Explain the roles within the project team and how they interact with one another. Emphasize the collaborative nature of the team and how each role contributes to the overall project success.
- **Responsibility Matrix:** Create a responsibility matrix (also known as a RACI chart) that defines who is Responsible, Accountable, Consulted, and Informed for each task or deliverable. This matrix clarifies decision-making and communication lines.
- **Document Roles and Responsibilities:** Record roles and responsibilities in a formal document such as a project charter, project management plan, or team handbook. Ensure that all team members have access to this document for reference.
- **Team Communication:** Establish open and clear communication channels among team members. Encourage regular updates, feedback, and information sharing to foster collaboration and transparency.
- **Clarify Expectations:** Clearly communicate the expectations for each role, including project deliverables, deadlines, and quality standards. Set SMART (Specific, Measurable, Achievable, Relevant, Time-bound) objectives for each team member.
- **Flexibility and Adaptability:** Acknowledge that roles and responsibilities may evolve as the project progresses or if circumstances change. Be flexible and ready to adjust roles to meet new challenges.
- **Address Role Overlaps and Gaps:** Identify any potential overlaps or gaps in roles and responsibilities. Ensure that there is no confusion or duplication of effort.
- **Support and Training:** Provide the necessary support, training, and resources for team members to fulfill their roles effectively. Offer guidance and mentorship where needed.
- **Monitor Performance:** Regularly assess individual and team performance against the defined roles and responsibilities. Provide feedback and recognition for a job well done.
- **Resolve Conflicts:** Address any conflicts or disagreements regarding roles and responsibilities promptly and constructively. Encourage open communication to resolve issues.

Understanding roles and responsibilities sets a solid foundation for project success. When team members are clear about their roles and how they contribute to the project's objectives, they can work together more effectively, stay motivated, and achieve better outcomes. Regularly review and update roles as needed to ensure alignment with project goals and changing project requirements.

Improving Team Communication & Collaboration

Improving team communication and collaboration is essential for enhancing productivity, fostering a positive team culture, and achieving successful project outcomes. Here are some strategies to improve team communication and collaboration:

- **Establish Clear Communication Channels:** Set up clear and efficient communication channels for the team to use. This may include team meetings, video conferences, instant messaging platforms, project management tools, and email. Choose channels that suit the team's preferences and needs.
- **Encourage Open and Transparent Communication:** Create a culture that values open and transparent communication. Encourage team members to share ideas, concerns, and progress updates freely. Foster an environment where everyone feels comfortable expressing their opinions.
- **Active Listening:** Emphasize the importance of active listening within the team. Encourage team members to attentively listen to one another's ideas and feedback. This ensures that everyone's input is heard and considered.
- **Regular Team Meetings:** Hold regular team meetings to discuss project progress, upcoming tasks, challenges, and successes. These meetings help keep everyone on the same page and provide an opportunity for collaboration and problem-solving.
- **Utilize Collaboration Tools:** Implement collaboration tools that facilitate teamwork and knowledge sharing. These tools may include shared document repositories, virtual whiteboards, and real-time editing platforms.
- **Clarify Roles and Responsibilities:** Ensure that team members have a clear understanding of their roles and responsibilities. This clarity helps in avoiding confusion and duplication of effort.
- **Set Clear Goals and Expectations:** Establish clear project goals and expectations for each team member. This clarity helps align efforts toward common objectives.
- **Promote Cross-Functional Collaboration:** Encourage collaboration between team members from different departments or areas of expertise. This cross-functional collaboration brings diverse perspectives to problem-solving and decision-making.
- **Celebrate Team Achievements:** Recognize and celebrate team achievements, both big and small. Acknowledging team efforts boosts morale and motivation.
- **Provide Constructive Feedback:** Offer constructive feedback to team members regularly. This feedback should be specific, actionable, and aimed at improvement. Encourage a culture of continuous learning and growth.
- **Manage Conflict Positively:** Address conflicts promptly and constructively. Create a safe space for resolving disagreements and encourage team members to find mutually beneficial solutions.
- **Team-Building Activities:** Organize team-building activities and events to strengthen relationships and build trust among team members. These activities can be both work-related and social in nature.
- **Lead by Example:** As a project manager or team lead, lead by example in promoting effective communication and collaboration. Be approachable, receptive to feedback, and demonstrate active engagement in team discussions.

Improving team communication and collaboration is an ongoing process. Regularly assess the effectiveness of communication strategies and seek feedback from team members. Adapt your approach as needed to create a positive and productive team environment. When team members feel connected and supported, they are more likely to work together harmoniously and achieve project success.

Resolving Conflicts Within the Team

Resolving conflicts within the team is crucial for maintaining a harmonious and productive work environment. Conflicts can arise due to differences in opinions, communication issues, competing priorities, or misunderstandings. As a project manager or team leader, it's essential to address conflicts promptly and constructively. Here are some steps to effectively resolve conflicts within the team:

- **Recognize the Conflict:** Be observant and attentive to identify signs of conflicts within the team. Address conflicts early before they escalate and negatively impact team dynamics.
- **Private Discussions:** Initiate private discussions with the individuals involved in the conflict. Create a safe and confidential space where team members can express their concerns and emotions freely.
- **Actively Listen:** Practice active listening during conflict discussions. Allow each person to express their viewpoint without interruptions. Show empathy and understanding to gain insight into the root causes of the conflict.
- **Identify the Underlying Issues:** Dig deeper to identify the underlying issues contributing to the conflict. Often, conflicts may be symptoms of more significant problems that need to be addressed.
- **Seek Common Ground:** Encourage the parties involved to find common ground and areas of agreement. Focus on shared goals and the project's success to foster collaboration.
- **Facilitate Communication:** Act as a neutral mediator to facilitate communication between conflicting parties. Ensure that everyone has an equal opportunity to express their perspectives.
- **Explore Solutions:** Brainstorm potential solutions together with the team members. Encourage creative problem-solving and explore win-win solutions that address the interests of all parties.
- **Establish Clear Expectations:** Clarify roles, responsibilities, and expectations to minimize future conflicts. Ensure that everyone is aware of their duties and how they contribute to the team's objectives.
- **Agree on Action Steps:** Reach a consensus on action steps to resolve the conflict. Assign responsibilities for implementing these steps and setting deadlines for resolution.
- **Follow Up:** Follow up with the team members to ensure that the agreed-upon solutions are being implemented and that progress is being made in resolving the conflict.
- **Encourage Collaboration:** Promote collaboration and teamwork within the team. Encourage team members to work together and support one another.
- **Maintain a Positive Team Culture:** Create a positive team culture that values open communication, respect, and constructive feedback. Address any behaviors that may contribute to conflicts.
- **Seek Mediation if Needed:** If the conflict persists or becomes challenging to resolve internally, consider seeking external mediation from a neutral third party.

Remember that conflicts are a natural part of any team dynamic. Resolving conflicts promptly and constructively can lead to better collaboration, stronger relationships, and increased productivity within the team. As a Project Manager or team leader your role is crucial in promoting a positive team environment and fostering effective conflict resolution.

With a well-organized and motivated project team, you are well-equipped to tackle the challenges that lie ahead. In this chapter, we have discussed the importance of team roles, communication, collaboration, and conflict resolution. By investing time and effort in building a strong and cohesive team, you increase the likelihood of project success and create a positive and rewarding work environment. In the next chapter, we will delve into the execution phase, where your project plans come to life, guided by your well-organized team.

Chapter 5: Executing the Project

Introduction: In this chapter, we delve into the exciting phase of executing the project. After thorough planning and organizing, it's time to put the project plan into action. This chapter outlines the key steps and best practices to ensure a smooth and successful project execution.

Kick-Off Meeting

- Organizing a project kick-off meeting to officially start the project.
- Introducing team members, stakeholders, and project objectives.
- Reviewing the project plan, timeline, roles, and responsibilities.
- Setting expectations and establishing a clear vision for project success.

Task Execution and Monitoring

- Assigning tasks to team members based on their roles and responsibilities.
- Implementing the project schedule and closely monitoring task progress.
- Addressing any deviations from the plan promptly and effectively.
- Encouraging proactive communication among team members to share updates and challenges.

Managing Resources

- Ensuring that resources, including human resources, equipment, and materials, are available as needed.
- Efficiently allocating resources to tasks and resolving resource conflicts.
- Tracking resource utilization and making adjustments and optimizing performance.

Stakeholder Communication

- Maintaining regular and transparent communication with stakeholders.
- Providing updates on project progress, milestones, and potential risks.
- Addressing stakeholder concerns and expectations proactively.

Quality Assurance

- Implementing quality control measures to ensure project deliverables meet the required standards.
- Conducting regular reviews and inspections to identify and rectify any defects.
- Monitoring customer feedback and making improvements as necessary.

Managing Changes

- Establishing a change control process to evaluate and approve any modifications to the project plan.
- Assessing the impact of proposed changes on scope, schedule, and resources.
- Communicating approved changes to the team and stakeholders.

Risk Management during Execution

- Continuously monitoring and reassessing project risks.
- Implementing risk response strategies to mitigate potential risks.
- Taking proactive measures to minimize the impact of unforeseen events.

Team Motivation and Engagement

- Keeping the team motivated and focused on project goals.
- Recognizing and rewarding team members for their efforts and achievements.
- Addressing any issues or concerns that may affect team morale.

Collaboration and Conflict Resolution

- Encouraging collaboration and open communication among team members.
- Resolving conflicts promptly and constructively to maintain a positive team environment.

Progress Reporting

- Preparing regular progress reports to keep stakeholders informed.
- Summarizing accomplishments, challenges, and upcoming milestones.
- Sharing lessons learned and improvements made during project execution.

The execution phase is the heart of the project, where the plans take shape and the team's efforts come to fruition. By effectively managing tasks, resources, and communication, project managers can lead the team to achieve project objectives successfully. In the next chapter, we will explore the critical process of project monitoring and control to ensure that the project stays on track and delivers the desired outcomes.

Implementing the Project Plan

Implementing your project plan is the core of the execution phase of the project, where the project team puts the carefully crafted plan into action. Successful implementation requires effective coordination, resource management, proactive problem-solving and risk mitigation planning. Here's a step-by-step guide on how to implement your project plan:

- **Kick-Off Meeting:** Hold a project kick-off meeting to officially start the execution phase. Review the project objectives, scope, roles, and responsibilities with the team and stakeholders. Set clear expectations and emphasize the importance of collaboration.
- **Task Assignment:** Assign tasks to team members based on their skills and expertise. Clearly communicate task details, deadlines, and expectations. Encourage ownership and accountability for each assigned task.
- **Resource Allocation:** Ensure that resources, including human resources, equipment, and materials, are allocated appropriately to support task execution. Monitor resource utilization and adjust, as needed, to maintain efficiency.
- **Communication and Collaboration:** Establish effective communication channels and encourage open collaboration among team members. Regularly share updates, progress, and challenges to keep everyone informed and aligned with project objectives.

- **Risk Management:** Continuously monitor project risks and implement risk response strategies to address potential issues. Be proactive in identifying and mitigating risks to minimize their impact on the project.
- **Quality Assurance:** Implement quality control measures to ensure that project deliverables meet the required standards. Regularly review and inspect work to identify and rectify any defects.
- **Change Management:** Establish a change control process to evaluate and approve any changes to the project plan. Assess the impact of proposed changes on scope, schedule, and resources before implementing them.
- **Stakeholder Engagement:** Maintain regular communication with stakeholders and provide updates on project progress. Address any stakeholder concerns or expectations promptly to maintain their support.
- **Monitor Progress:** Regularly monitor the progress of tasks and milestones against the project schedule. Use project management tools or software to track project status and identify any deviations from the plan.
- **Address Issues and Challenges:** Address issues or challenges that arise during implementation promptly and effectively. Encourage a problem-solving mindset within the team to overcome obstacles.
- **Team Motivation:** Keep the team motivated and engaged throughout the project. Recognize and reward team members for their efforts and achievements. Provide support and encouragement to boost morale.
- **Documentation:** Maintain comprehensive project documentation, including meeting minutes, progress reports, and any changes or decisions made during implementation.
- **Adaptability:** Be adaptable to changes or unforeseen events that may impact the project. Adjust the plan as needed to stay on track with project objectives.
- **Regular Review Meetings:** Conduct regular review meetings with the team and stakeholders to assess progress, discuss challenges, and ensure alignment with project goals.
- **Celebrate Milestones:** Celebrate project milestones and achievements as they are reached. Acknowledge the team's hard work and dedication.

By following these steps and maintaining a proactive approach, project managers can effectively implement the detailed project plan, navigate challenges, and lead the team toward successful project completion. Regular communication, collaboration, and monitoring are key to ensuring that the project stays on track and delivers the desired outcomes.

Monitoring Project Progress & Performance

Monitoring project progress and performance is a critical aspect of project management. It involves regularly assessing the project's status, comparing actual progress against the project plan, and making necessary adjustments to keep the project on track. Here's how to effectively monitor project progress and performance:

- **Establish Key Performance Indicators (KPIs):** Define specific KPIs that measure the project's performance and success. KPIs may include milestones achieved, budget utilization, schedule adherence, quality metrics, customer satisfaction, and more.
- **Use Project Management Software:** Leverage project management software or tools to track and manage project progress. These tools provide real-time insights into task status, resource allocation, and overall project health.
- **Regular Progress Updates:** Hold regular status update meetings with the project team to discuss progress, challenges, and upcoming tasks. Use these meetings to address any issues and ensure everyone is aligned with the project objectives.
- **Gantt Charts and Project Dashboards:** Utilize Gantt charts and project dashboards to visualize project timelines and progress. These tools provide a clear overview of task dependencies, critical paths, and potential delays.

- **Document Changes and Deviations:** Keep a record of any changes to the project plan and deviations from the original schedule or scope. Documenting changes helps in assessing their impact and making informed decisions.
- **Compare Actual vs. Planned Progress:** Regularly compare actual progress against the planned schedule and milestones. Identify any delays or deviations and take corrective actions promptly.
- **Risk Monitoring:** Continuously assess project risks and their potential impact on the project. Implement risk response strategies to mitigate risks as they arise.
- **Quality Assurance and Control:** Regularly review project deliverables to ensure they meet the required quality standards. Conduct inspections and quality checks to identify and address any defects.
- **Budget Tracking:** Monitor project expenditures and resource utilization against the budget. Implement cost control measures to avoid budget overruns.
- **Stakeholder Communication:** Keep stakeholders informed about project progress through regular updates, progress reports, and status meetings. Address any concerns or queries they may have.
- **Team Performance Evaluation:** Evaluate team performance against individual and collective goals. Provide feedback and coaching to support team members' professional growth.
- **Lessons Learned:** Document lessons learned throughout the project. Analyze successes and challenges to identify areas for improvement in future projects.
- **Proactive Problem-Solving:** Be proactive in identifying and addressing potential issues before they escalate. Encourage a problem-solving approach within the team.
- **Stay Agile:** Be open to adjustments and changes during the project's execution. Adaptability is key to responding effectively to evolving project requirements.
- **Regularly Review Project Plan:** Review and update the project plan as needed to reflect changes and lessons learned during project monitoring.

By diligently monitoring project progress and performance, project managers can identify and address issues early, maintain control over the project's trajectory, and deliver successful outcomes. Regular communication and collaboration among team members and stakeholders are vital for effective monitoring and overall project success.

Managing Changes & Unexpected Issues

Managing changes and unexpected issues is a critical aspect of project management, as no project is immune to uncertainties or modifications in requirements. Being prepared to handle changes and issues in a structured manner is essential for maintaining project success. Here's how to effectively manage changes and unexpected issues during the project:

- **Change Control Process:** Establish a change control process to evaluate and approve any proposed changes to the project plan. This process should involve assessing the impact of changes on scope, schedule, resources, and budget before making decisions.
- **Change Request Form:** Require stakeholders to submit change requests through a standardized form. This form should include details such as the reason for the change, the impact on the project, and proposed solutions.
- **Impact Analysis:** Conduct a thorough impact analysis of proposed changes to understand their implications on project objectives, resources, and timeline. Consider potential risks and benefits associated with each change.
- **Change Review Board:** Form a change review board or committee comprising relevant stakeholders to evaluate change requests objectively. The board should consist of representatives from different areas to ensure comprehensive assessment.
- **Prioritization of Changes:** Prioritize change requests based on their urgency, impact on project success, and alignment with strategic objectives. Address high-priority changes promptly while considering the capacity to accommodate multiple changes simultaneously.
- **Communication and Approval:** Communicate proposed changes and their impact to stakeholders, including team members, clients, and management. Seek approval from the appropriate authority before implementing any changes.

- **Contingency Planning:** Develop contingency plans to address unexpected issues that may arise during the project. Anticipate potential risks and have predefined strategies in place to manage them.
- **Adaptability and Flexibility:** Remain adaptable and flexible in response to unexpected issues. Be prepared to adjust the project plan as necessary without compromising the overall project objectives.
- **Risk Management:** Maintain a proactive risk management approach to identify and mitigate potential issues before they escalate. Regularly review and update the risk register.
- **Team Collaboration:** Encourage open communication and collaboration among team members when addressing unexpected issues. Foster a problem-solving mindset and facilitate brainstorming sessions to find creative solutions.
- **Continuous Monitoring:** Continuously monitor project progress and performance to detect early signs of potential issues. Promptly address any deviations from the plan.
- **Lessons Learned:** Document lessons learned from previous projects or similar situations. Apply these insights to address issues effectively and make informed decisions.
- **Maintain Stakeholder Engagement:** Keep stakeholders informed about changes and unexpected issues. Engage them in the decision-making process and ensure their support throughout the resolution.
- **Record Keeping:** Maintain comprehensive documentation of all changes made, decisions taken, and their outcomes. This record helps in post-project evaluations and provides valuable insights for future projects.

By effectively managing changes and unexpected issues, project managers demonstrate their ability to adapt and ensure project success despite evolving circumstances. Emphasize proactive planning, clear communication, collaboration, and adherence to established processes to maintain control over the project's progress and deliver positive outcomes.

Delivering On-time & Within Budget

Delivering a project on-time and within budget is a challenging but essential goal for project managers. It requires careful planning, efficient resource management, and proactive problem-solving. Here are some strategies to increase the likelihood of delivering a project on-time and within budget:

- **Thorough Planning:** Invest sufficient time in the planning phase to define project objectives, scope, deliverables, and a realistic timeline. A well-structured project plan serves as a roadmap for successful execution.
- **Scope Management:** Clearly define the project scope and resist scope creep. Any changes to the scope should go through a formal change control process with a thorough impact analysis.
- **Resource Allocation:** Carefully allocate resources, including human resources, equipment, and materials, based on project requirements. Avoid overloading team members with multiple projects.
- **Time Estimation:** Accurately estimate the time required for each task and milestone. Involve relevant team members in the estimation process to gain more realistic insights.
- **Risk Management:** Proactively identify potential risks and develop risk response strategies. Regularly assess and monitor risks throughout the project to minimize their impact.
- **Contingency Planning:** Have contingency plans in place to address unforeseen events or delays. Include buffer time and resources in the project plan to accommodate unexpected challenges.
- **Regular Monitoring and Control:** Monitor project progress and performance regularly against the project plan. Use project management tools to track tasks and milestones and make necessary adjustments.
- **Communication and Collaboration:** Maintain open and transparent communication among team members and stakeholders. Foster collaboration and teamwork to resolve issues collectively.

- **Performance Evaluation:** Regularly evaluate team performance and individual contributions. Provide feedback and support to enhance productivity and motivation.
- **Cost Management:** Monitor project expenses and resource utilization. Implement cost control measures to stay within the approved budget.
- **Vendor Management:** If applicable, effectively manage relationships with external vendors or contractors to ensure timely delivery and quality work.
- **Client Engagement:** Keep clients or stakeholders informed about project progress and any potential changes. Seek their feedback and involvement throughout the project.
- **Learning from Past Projects:** Analyze lessons learned from previous projects and apply them to improve efficiency and decision-making in the current project.
- **Adaptability:** Be flexible and adaptable to changes or unforeseen events. Adjust the project plan as needed without compromising the project's core objectives.
- **Proactive Issue Resolution:** Address project issues promptly and proactively. Encourage the team to identify and resolve challenges before they escalate.

By employing these strategies and maintaining a proactive and collaborative approach, project managers can increase the likelihood of delivering projects on-time and within budget. A well-managed project not only achieves its objectives but also strengthens the team's capabilities and client relationships, contributing to long-term success.

Chapter 6: Managing Project Risks

In this chapter, we delve into the critical process of managing project risks. Risk management is a systematic approach to identifying, analyzing, and addressing potential uncertainties that could impact project objectives. By effectively managing risks, project managers can minimize threats and capitalize on opportunities, increasing the likelihood of project success.

Risk Identification

- Understanding the concept of risk and its significance in project management.
- Techniques for identifying project risks, including brainstorming, risk checklists, lessons learned, and expert judgment.
- Categorizing risks into different types, such as technical, external, organizational, and market risks.

Risk Assessment and Analysis

- Evaluating the likelihood and impact of identified risks on project objectives.
- Prioritizing risks based on their severity and potential consequences.
- Conducting qualitative and quantitative risk analysis to assess risks comprehensively.

Risk Response Strategies

- Developing risk response strategies to address different types of risks.
- Strategies for handling negative risks (threats) include avoidance, mitigation, transfer, and acceptance.
- Strategies for addressing positive risks (opportunities) include exploitation, enhancement, sharing, and acceptance.

Risk Mitigation and Contingency Planning

- Implementing risk mitigation measures to reduce the probability and impact of identified risks.
- Developing contingency plans to address high-impact risks if they occur.
- Allocating resources and defining responsibilities for risk mitigation and contingency actions.

Risk Monitoring and Control

- Establishing a risk monitoring and control process to track the status of identified risks.
- Regularly reviewing risk registers and updating risk assessments as needed.
- Implementing risk response actions and evaluating their effectiveness.

Communication and Reporting

- Communicating risk-related information to stakeholders, including project team members and management.

- Presenting risk assessments and mitigation strategies in a clear and understandable manner.
- Reporting on risk management progress and outcomes regularly.

Risk Culture and Awareness

- Creating a risk-aware culture within the project team and organization.
- Encouraging proactive risk identification and reporting at all levels.
- Providing training and resources to enhance risk management skills.

Continuous Improvement

- Conducting post-project risk assessments to identify lessons learned and areas for improvement.
- Integrating risk management experiences into future projects.
- Continuously refining risk management processes based on feedback and outcomes.

Effective risk management is a dynamic and iterative process that requires vigilance and collaboration. By proactively addressing risks throughout the project lifecycle, project managers can increase project resilience and deliver successful outcomes. In the next chapter, we will explore the crucial process of project communication, which underpins successful project execution and stakeholder engagement.

Identifying Potential Risk

Identifying potential risk is a critical step in the risk management process. It involves systematically recognizing uncertainties that could impact project objectives, both negatively (threats) and positively (opportunities). Here are some techniques and approaches to identify potential risks in a project:

- **Brainstorming:** Conduct brainstorming sessions with the project team and stakeholders to generate a list of potential risks. Encourage open discussions to explore various scenarios and perspectives.
- **Risk Checklists:** Use risk checklists that are specific to the project's industry or domain. These checklists serve as guides to prompt the identification of common risks relevant to the project.
- **Lessons Learned:** Review lessons learned from past projects to identify risks that were encountered and addressed in previous endeavors. This can provide valuable insights into potential risks for the current project.
- **SWOT Analysis:** Perform a SWOT (Strengths, Weaknesses, Opportunities, Threats) analysis to identify internal and external factors that could impact the project positively or negatively.
- **Expert Judgment:** Seek input from subject matter experts and experienced individuals in relevant fields. Their expertise can help identify risks that might not be apparent to the project team.
- **Assumptions Analysis:** Review the assumptions made during project planning. Identify any assumptions that could pose risks if they are not valid or change during the project.
- **Risk Registers:** Consult historical risk registers from previous projects within the organization to identify recurring risks or patterns.
- **External Factors:** Consider external factors such as market trends, regulatory changes, economic conditions, and geopolitical events that may affect the project.
- **Dependencies and Interfaces:** Examine dependencies between tasks and interfaces with other projects, departments, or external parties. Disruptions in these areas could pose risks.
- **Stakeholder Analysis:** Understand the concerns and objectives of key stakeholders. This helps identify risks related to conflicting expectations or resistance to change.
- **SWOT Analysis:** Perform a SWOT (Strengths, Weaknesses, Opportunities, Threats) analysis to identify internal and external factors that could impact the project positively or negatively.
- **Industry Research:** Conduct research on industry-specific risks and best practices to identify risks common to projects in the same domain.

- **Risk Workshops:** Organize risk workshops involving cross-functional teams to identify risks from various perspectives and expertise.
- **Project Reviews:** Regularly review project documentation, progress reports, and status updates to identify emerging risks or trends.
- **Environmental Scanning:** Stay updated on current events, emerging technologies, and market shifts that may introduce new risks or opportunities to the project.

Remember that risk identification is an ongoing process throughout the project lifecycle. Encourage open communication and a risk-aware culture within the project team and organization to ensure potential risks are continuously identified and managed effectively.

Analyzing & Prioritizing Risks

Analyzing and prioritizing risks are essential steps in the risk management process. It involves assessing the identified risks to understand their potential impact on the project's objectives and determining which risks require immediate attention. Here's how to analyze and prioritize risks effectively:

- **Risk Assessment Matrix:** Create a risk assessment matrix to evaluate each risk based on its likelihood of occurrence and potential impact on project objectives. Assign a numerical value to both factors and calculate a risk score for each identified risk.
- **Qualitative Risk Analysis:** Conduct qualitative risk analysis to subjectively assess the significance of risks. Use techniques such as probability and impact assessment, risk categorization, and risk urgency assessment to prioritize risks.
- **Quantitative Risk Analysis:** For high-impact or complex projects, consider quantitative risk analysis. Use statistical methods, sensitivity analysis, or Monte Carlo simulation to quantify the probability of risk occurrence and potential impacts on project outcomes.
- **Risk Ranking:** Rank risks based on their risk scores or qualitative assessments. This ranking helps in identifying the most critical risks that need immediate attention.
- **Risk Triage:** Divide the risks into three categories: high, medium, and low priority. High-priority risks require immediate attention and specific risk response strategies. Medium-priority risks may need further monitoring, while low-priority risks may be accepted without further action.
- **Risk Urgency Assessment:** Assess the urgency of addressing each risk. Some risks may have long-term impacts, while others require immediate action to prevent serious consequences.
- **Risk Response Planning:** Based on the risk analysis and prioritization, develop appropriate risk response plans for high-priority risks. Determine the best strategies to address each risk, such as risk avoidance, risk mitigation, risk transfer, or risk acceptance.
- **Risk Appetite and Tolerance:** Consider the organization's risk appetite and tolerance levels when prioritizing risks. Align risk management efforts with the organization's overall risk strategy.
- **Communication with Stakeholders:** Communicate the results of risk analysis and prioritization to stakeholders, including project team members, management, and clients. Ensure a shared understanding of the project's most significant risks and the proposed response strategies.
- **Reassessing Risks:** Perform periodic reviews of risk analysis and prioritization throughout the project lifecycle. New risks may emerge, and the impact of existing risks may change, requiring updates to the risk management approach.
- **Documentation:** Maintain a comprehensive risk register documenting all identified risks, their analysis, prioritization, and the corresponding risk response plans. This register serves as a valuable reference throughout the project.
- **Continuous Improvement:** Regularly evaluate the effectiveness of risk analysis and prioritization processes. Incorporate lessons learned from previous projects to refine risk management practices in future endeavors.

By carefully analyzing and prioritizing risks, project managers can allocate resources and attention where they are most needed, ensuring that critical risks are adequately managed and potential opportunities are capitalized upon. A systematic approach to risk analysis strengthens the project's resilience and enhances the chances of successful project outcomes.

Creating Risk Response/Mitigation Plans

Creating risk response plans is a crucial step in the risk management process. Risk response plans outline specific actions to address identified risks, mitigating their potential negative impact on the project. Here's a systematic approach to creating risk response plans:

- **Review Risk Analysis:** Refer to the results of risk analysis and prioritization to identify high-priority risks that require immediate attention and response planning.
- **Define Objectives:** Clearly define the objectives of the risk response plan. Determine the desired outcome of addressing each risk, whether it's to avoid, mitigate, transfer, or accept the risk.
- **Identify Response Strategies:** Select appropriate risk response strategies for each identified risk based on its nature and the organization's risk tolerance. The response strategies can include:
  - **Avoidance:** Taking actions to eliminate the risk entirely, such as changing the project scope or approach.
  - **Mitigation:** Implementing measures to reduce the probability or impact of the risk.
  - **Transfer:** Shifting the responsibility for the risk to a third party, such as through insurance or outsourcing.
  - **Acceptance:** Acknowledging the risk and its potential impact without taking further action.
- **Develop Action Plans:** For each selected response strategy, develop detailed action plans outlining the steps to be taken. Specify who will be responsible for each action, the timeline, and the required resources.
- **Allocate Resources:** Ensure that adequate resources, including budget, time, and expertise, are allocated to implement the risk response plans effectively.
- **Integration with Project Plan:** Integrate the risk response plans into the overall project plan and schedule. Ensure that they align with project milestones and activities.
- **Contingency Planning:** For high-impact risks with a significant probability of occurrence, develop contingency plans. Contingency plans outline alternative actions to be taken if the risk materializes.
- **Testing and Simulations:** Consider conducting testing or simulations to validate the effectiveness of the risk response plans and identify any potential gaps or weaknesses.
- **Communication and Training:** Communicate the risk response plans to all relevant stakeholders, including the project team, management, and clients. Ensure that everyone understands their roles and responsibilities in implementing the plans.
- **Document and Maintain:** Document all risk response plans in the risk register or a separate risk management document. Regularly update the plans as needed throughout the project.
- **Continuous Monitoring:** Continuously monitor the implementation of risk response plans and the effectiveness of the actions taken. Be prepared to adjust the plans if circumstances change.
- **Lessons Learned:** After the project, conduct a lesson's learned session to evaluate the success of the risk response plans. Identify areas of improvement for future projects based on what went well and other areas where you know improvement is required.

By proactively creating risk response plans, project managers can effectively address potential risks and increase the project's chances of success. A well-executed risk response plan minimizes the negative impact of uncertainties and allows the project team to focus on achieving project objectives efficiently. We always need to learn from what went right but just as important what didn't go as well as planned. The best project managers will consistently analyze strengths and areas for opportunity and will always get better and set themselves apart from the others.

Continuous Risk Monitoring & Mitigation

Continuous risk monitoring and mitigation is a vital part of effective risk management. It involves ongoing surveillance of identified risks, as well as new risks that may emerge during the project. By actively monitoring and promptly addressing risks, project managers can minimize their potential impact and maintain project success. Here's how to implement continuous risk monitoring and mitigation:

- **Regular Risk Reviews:** Schedule regular risk review meetings to assess the status of identified risks. Review the risk register and update it as needed with new risks or changes to existing ones.
- **Risk Trigger Identification:** Identify triggers or early warning signs that indicate a risk is becoming more likely or its impact is increasing. Establish thresholds for risk triggers that signal the need for action.
- **Risk Ownership:** Assign specific team members as risk owners who are responsible for monitoring and managing individual risks. Empower them to take proactive actions as needed.
- **Key Performance Indicators (KPIs):** Establish KPIs related to risk management to measure the effectiveness of risk mitigation efforts. Monitor these KPIs regularly to track progress.
- **Real-time Data Tracking:** Utilize project management tools and software to track real-time data on project performance and potential risk indicators. This enables timely responses to emerging risks.
- **Stakeholder Engagement:** Engage stakeholders throughout the project to gather their insights and perspectives on potential risks. Their feedback can help identify risks that may be overlooked.
- **Scenario Planning:** Conduct scenario planning exercises to assess the impact of different risk scenarios on the project. Develop contingency plans for high-impact risks.
- **Risk Reporting:** Generate regular risk reports and share them with relevant stakeholders. Present the status of identified risks, response actions taken, and any changes in risk likelihood or impact.
- **Lessons Learned:** Incorporate lessons learned from previous projects into risk monitoring and mitigation efforts. Apply successful risk management practices and avoid previous pitfalls.
- **Training and Awareness:** Provide training to the project team on risk management best practices. Raise awareness of the importance of risk monitoring and how each team member can contribute.
- **Collaboration and Communication:** Foster a culture of collaboration and open communication among team members. Encourage sharing of risk-related information and prompt reporting of potential risks.
- **Risk-Response Flexibility:** Be prepared to adapt risk response strategies based on changing circumstances or new information. Flexibility is crucial for effective risk management.
- **Continuous Improvement:** Continuously review and improve risk management processes based on project experiences. Implement feedback and suggestions to enhance risk management practices.
- **Risk Review during Project Updates:** Incorporate risk review and mitigation updates in regular project status meetings. Discuss the status of identified risks and any new risks that have emerged.

By integrating continuous risk monitoring and mitigation into the project's day-to-day activities, project managers can stay proactive in managing uncertainties. This approach empowers the team to identify and address potential risks early, ensuring that the project remains on track and delivers the desired outcomes.

Chapter 7: Quality Control & Assurance

In this chapter, we explore the critical aspects of quality control and assurance in project management. Quality is a key determinant of project success and ensuring that deliverables meet or exceed the required standards is essential to meet stakeholder expectations. Quality control focuses on inspecting and validating project outputs, while quality assurance focuses on implementing processes and practices to enhance overall project quality.

Understanding Quality in Project Management

- Defining quality in the context of project management.
- Recognizing the importance of quality in achieving project objectives and stakeholder satisfaction.
- Differentiating between quality control and quality assurance and their roles in project success.

Developing a Quality Management Plan

- Creating a comprehensive quality management plan that outlines how quality will be achieved and maintained throughout the project.
- Identifying quality objectives, standards, and criteria for project deliverables.
- Defining roles and responsibilities for quality control and assurance activities.

Quality Planning and Standards

- Planning for quality at the project initiation phase.
- Setting clear quality standards for project deliverables in collaboration with stakeholders.
- Establishing quality metrics and acceptance criteria to measure project performance.

Quality Control Activities

- Implementing quality control processes to verify project outputs against predefined quality standards.
- Performing inspections, reviews, and tests to identify defects or deviations.
- Taking corrective actions to address identified quality issues.

Quality Assurance Processes

- Integrating quality assurance practices into the project life cycle.
- Conducting audits and process reviews to evaluate compliance with established quality procedures.
- Identifying areas for improvement and implementing preventive actions to enhance quality.

Continuous Improvement and Lessons Learned

- Emphasizing a culture of continuous improvement throughout the project.
- Conducting regular lessons learned sessions to identify successes and areas for quality enhancement.

- Incorporating lessons learned into future projects to enhance overall project performance.

Stakeholder Communication and Engagement

- Communicating quality-related information to stakeholders proactively.
- Involving stakeholders in quality planning and decision-making processes.
- Addressing stakeholder concerns related to project quality.

Training and Skill Development

- Providing training and development opportunities to enhance team members' skills in delivering high-quality results.
- Promoting awareness of the importance of quality among all project stakeholders.

Quality control and assurance are indispensable components of project management. By implementing robust quality practices, project managers can ensure that project deliverables meet the required standards and align with stakeholder expectations. In the next chapter, we will explore the crucial aspect of project communication, which plays a pivotal role in successful project execution and stakeholder engagement.

Understanding Quality in Project Deliverables

Understanding quality in project deliverables is crucial for project success. Quality refers to the degree to which project outputs meet the specified requirements and expectations of stakeholders. It goes beyond just meeting technical specifications; it encompasses factors like reliability, performance, usability, and customer satisfaction. Here are key aspects of understanding quality in project deliverables:

- **Meeting Requirements:** Quality deliverables must align with the project's defined requirements and objectives. They should fulfill the needs and expectations of stakeholders, including clients, end-users, and management.
- **Fitness for Purpose:** Deliverables must be fit for their intended purpose and perform their intended functions effectively. They should be designed to address the project's specific goals and solve the identified problems.
- **Consistency and Uniformity:** Deliverables should exhibit consistency and uniformity across all components. They should adhere to standard practices, guidelines, and design principles.
- **Accuracy and Precision:** Deliverables should be accurate, free from errors, and precise in their execution. Any data, calculations, or measurements must be reliable and verifiable.
- **Completeness and Comprehensiveness:** Quality deliverables should be complete and include all required components. They should provide comprehensive solutions and cover all aspects necessary for successful implementation.
- **Timeliness:** Deliverables should be provided within the agreed-upon timelines and milestones. Timeliness is critical to project scheduling and meeting stakeholder expectations.
- **Reliability and Durability:** Deliverables should be reliable and durable, able to perform as expected over the project's intended lifespan. They should withstand normal usage and environmental conditions.
- **Ease of Use:** User-friendliness is an essential aspect of quality in project deliverables. They should be easy to use, intuitive, and require minimal training or support.
- **Scalability and Flexibility:** Quality deliverables should be scalable to accommodate future growth or changes. They should be flexible enough to adapt to evolving requirements.
- **Adherence to Standards and Regulations:** Deliverables must comply with relevant industry standards, regulations, and legal requirements. Non-compliance can lead to legal and financial consequences.

- **Customer Satisfaction:** The ultimate measure of quality is customer satisfaction. Deliverables should meet or exceed customer expectations and address their needs effectively.
- **Peer Review and Validation:** Quality deliverables often undergo peer reviews and validation processes. Independent assessments help identify potential issues and ensure high quality.
- **Continuous Improvement:** Quality is an ongoing commitment. Project teams should continuously strive to improve deliverables based on feedback, lessons learned, and emerging best practices.
- **Risk Management:** Addressing quality risks is crucial. Proactively identifying and mitigating risks related to deliverables can prevent quality issues and rework.

By understanding and emphasizing quality in project deliverables, project managers can ensure that the final outputs meet stakeholder expectations, leading to successful project outcomes and customer satisfaction. A robust quality management approach enhances the project's reputation, builds trust with stakeholders, and improves the organization's overall competitiveness.

Developing A Quality Management Plan

Developing a Quality Management Plan is a critical step in ensuring that project deliverables meet the required standards and stakeholder expectations. The Quality Management Plan outlines the processes, procedures, and activities that will be implemented throughout the project to achieve and maintain high-quality outcomes. Here's a step-by-step guide to developing a Quality Management Plan:

- **Understand Project Requirements:** Gather and review all project requirements and objectives. Understand the quality expectations of stakeholders and any specific quality standards that must be met.
- **Identify Quality Objectives:** Define clear and measurable quality objectives that align with the project's goals. These objectives will serve as the foundation for all quality-related activities.
- **Identify Quality Standards and Criteria:** Determine the quality standards that will be applied to project deliverables. These standards can be based on industry best practices, organizational policies, or regulatory requirements. Establish clear acceptance criteria for each deliverable.
- **Assign Roles and Responsibilities:** Identify the individuals or teams responsible for quality control and assurance activities. Assign roles such as Quality Manager, Quality Assurance Team, and Quality Control Inspectors.
- **Quality Control Processes:** Detail the quality control processes that will be used to inspect project deliverables and ensure they meet the defined quality standards. Include procedures for identifying defects, non-conformities, and corrective actions.
- **Quality Assurance Processes:** Outline the quality assurance processes that will be implemented to ensure that the project's overall quality management approach is effective and efficient. This includes conducting audits, process reviews, and performance evaluations.
- **Resource Allocation:** Identify the resources (human, financial, and technological) required to implement the quality management plan successfully. Ensure that adequate resources are allocated to each quality-related activity.
- **Risk Management:** Include risk management strategies in the Quality Management Plan. Address potential risks that may impact project quality and define risk response actions.
- **Training and Skill Development:** Specify any training or skill development initiatives needed to enhance team members' capabilities in delivering high-quality work.
- **Documentation and Reporting:** Define the documentation requirements for quality-related activities, including record-keeping, inspection reports, and audit findings. Establish a reporting mechanism to communicate quality-related information to stakeholders.
- **Communication with Stakeholders:** Detail the approach for communicating quality-related information to project stakeholders, including clients, management, and the project team.
- **Continuous Improvement:** Outline how continuous improvement will be fostered throughout the project. Include processes for capturing lessons learned and implementing improvements based on feedback.

- **Integration with Project Plan:** Integrate the Quality Management Plan with the overall project plan to ensure that quality-related activities are aligned with project milestones and timelines.
- **Review and Approval:** Seek input from key stakeholders and project team members and obtain their approval for the Quality Management Plan.
- **Implementation and Execution:** After approval, implement and execute the Quality Management Plan throughout the project lifecycle. Regularly review and update the plan as needed.

By developing a comprehensive Quality Management Plan, project managers can systematically ensure that all project deliverables meet the required standards and contribute to the overall success of the project. A focus on quality enhances the project's reputation, builds trust with stakeholders, and leads to higher levels of customer satisfaction.

Conducting Quality Assurance & Control Activities

Conducting quality assurance and control activities is essential to ensure that project deliverables meet the defined quality standards and stakeholder expectations. Quality assurance focuses on implementing processes and practices to enhance overall project quality, while quality control involves inspecting and validating project outputs for compliance with quality standards. Here's a step-by-step guide to conducting quality assurance and control activities:

- **Quality Assurance Activities:**
    - **Establish Quality Assurance Processes:** Define the procedures and guidelines for quality assurance activities, including audits, reviews, and performance evaluations.
    - **Conduct Process Audits:** Regularly review project processes and workflows to ensure they adhere to established quality standards and best practices.
    - **Verify Documentation:** Check that project documentation, including plans, requirements, and design documents, is accurate, complete, and up-to-date.
    - **Monitor Quality Metrics:** Continuously monitor key quality metrics to track project performance and identify areas for improvement.
    - **Conduct Performance Reviews:** Evaluate the performance of project team members and subcontractors to ensure they meet quality expectations.
    - **Implement Corrective Actions:** Address any identified issues or non-conformities promptly by implementing corrective actions.
- **Quality Control Activities:**
    - **Define Acceptance Criteria:** Establish clear acceptance criteria for each project deliverable based on predefined quality standards and stakeholder requirements.
    - **Perform Inspections:** Conduct inspections and reviews of project deliverables at various stages to identify defects and ensure compliance with quality standards.
    - **Use Quality Checklists:** Utilize quality checklists to guide inspections and verify that all required elements are present in the deliverables.
    - **Test Deliverables:** Perform testing, as appropriate, to verify the functionality, performance, and reliability of the deliverables.

- **Validate Data and Results:** Verify the accuracy and validity of data used in the project deliverables to ensure reliable outcomes.
- **Address Non-Conformities:** If any deliverable fails to meet the acceptance criteria, take corrective actions to rectify the issues.
- **Document Control:** Manage project documentation and versions to avoid inconsistencies and ensure that the latest approved versions are being used.

- **Continuous Improvement:**
  - **Encourage Feedback:** Foster a culture of continuous improvement by seeking feedback from stakeholders, team members, and end-users.
  - **Capture Lessons Learned:** Regularly capture lessons learned from quality assurance and control activities. Use these insights to improve future project processes.
  - **Implement Best Practices:** Apply successful quality practices from previous projects to enhance the current project's performance.
  - **Adapt to Changing Requirements:** Stay flexible and adapt quality processes to align with changing project requirements and stakeholder expectations.

- **Communication With Stakeholders:**
  - **Communicate Quality Results:** Regularly communicate quality assurance and control findings to relevant stakeholders, including project progress and outcomes.
  - **Address Stakeholder Concerns:** Address any quality-related concerns raised by stakeholders promptly and transparently.
  - **Document & Records**
  - Maintain Quality Records: Keep comprehensive records of all quality assurance and control activities, including inspection reports, audit findings, and test results.
  - **Generate Quality Reports:** Provide periodic quality reports to stakeholders to demonstrate the project's adherence to quality standards.

By conducting thorough quality assurance and control activities, project managers can ensure that project deliverables meet the required quality standards, leading to increased stakeholder satisfaction and successful project outcomes. A proactive approach to quality management enhances the project's reputation, strengthens stakeholder confidence, and contributes to the overall success of the organization.

Ensuring Customer Satisfaction

Ensuring customer satisfaction is a critical aspect of successful project management. Satisfied customers are more likely to provide positive feedback, continue doing business with the organization, and recommend its services to others. Here are key strategies to ensure customer satisfaction throughout the project:

- **Clear Communication:** Maintain open and transparent communication with customers throughout the project. Clearly convey project progress, milestones, and any changes that may impact the customer.
- **Engage Customers in Planning:** Involve customers in project planning to gather their input and align project objectives with their expectations. Understand their needs and preferences.
- **Set Realistic Expectations:** Set achievable project goals and manage customer expectations appropriately. Avoid overpromising and underdelivering.
- **Regular Updates:** Provide regular updates on project status, achievements, and potential challenges. Keep customers informed to build trust and confidence.
- **Quality Deliverables:** Deliver high-quality project outputs that meet or exceed customer expectations. Ensure that deliverables are reliable, accurate, and free from defects.
- **Proactive Issue Resolution:** Address any issues or concerns raised by customers promptly and proactively. Demonstrate a commitment to resolving problems to their satisfaction.
- **Customer Feedback:** Solicit feedback from customers at various stages of the project. Act on feedback to improve project performance and customer experience.
- **Measure Customer Satisfaction:** Implement surveys or feedback mechanisms to assess customer satisfaction. Analyze the results and use insights to enhance project delivery.
- **Personalized Service:** Tailor project delivery to the unique needs and preferences of individual customers. Offer personalized support and attention.
- **Adaptability:** Be flexible and adaptable to accommodate changes or additional requests from customers when possible.
- **On-Time Delivery:** Strive to meet project deadlines and deliver on time. Communicate proactively if any delays are anticipated.
- **Exceed Expectations:** Look for opportunities to go above and beyond in delivering value to customers. Surprise them with exceptional service or features they did not expect.
- **Post-Project Follow-Up:** Follow up with customers after project completion to ensure their satisfaction and address any post-implementation issues.
- **Customer Service Excellence:** Cultivate a customer-centric culture within the project team and organization. Train team members to provide excellent customer service.
- **Learn from Feedback:** Use customer feedback, both positive and negative, as a learning opportunity. Implement improvements based on lessons learned.
- **Celebrate Successes:** Acknowledge project successes and celebrate milestones with customers. Demonstrate appreciation for their partnership.

By focusing on customer satisfaction throughout the project lifecycle, project managers can foster long-term relationships with clients, increase loyalty, and position the organization as a preferred service provider. Satisfied customers are more likely to provide repeat business and serve as brand advocates, contributing to the organization's overall success and growth.

Chapter 8: Communication and Reporting

Effective communication and reporting are critical components of successful project management. In this chapter, we explore the importance of clear and timely communication with stakeholders and the significance of regular project reporting. Proper communication ensures that project teams stay aligned, stakeholders are informed, and potential issues are addressed promptly.

Understanding Communication in Project Management

- The role of communication in project success.
- Identifying project communication stakeholders and their information needs.
- Overcoming communication barriers and challenges.

Developing a Communication Plan

- Creating a comprehensive communication plan that outlines the communication objectives, methods, frequency, and responsible parties.
- Identifying the key messages to be communicated to various stakeholders.
- Tailoring communication approaches to suit different stakeholder preferences.

Effective Project Meetings

- Planning and conducting productive project meetings.
- Setting clear agendas and objectives for meetings.
- Facilitating discussions and encouraging active participation.

Project Status Reporting

- Establishing a standardized project reporting structure.
- Defining key performance indicators (KPIs) to measure project progress.
- Creating concise and informative project status reports.

Risk Communication

- Communicating project risks and mitigation strategies to stakeholders.
- Addressing stakeholder concerns related to project risks.
- Building trust through transparent risk communication.

Change Management Communication

- Communicating changes to project scope, schedule, or resources effectively.
- Managing stakeholder expectations during periods of change.
- Mitigating resistance to change through clear and persuasive communication.

Conflict Resolution and Communication

- Dealing with conflicts and disagreements among project team members or stakeholders.
- Employing effective communication techniques to resolve conflicts.
- Promoting a positive and collaborative team environment.

Stakeholder Engagement

- Engaging stakeholders throughout the project lifecycle.
- Establishing feedback channels and incorporating stakeholder input into decision-making.
- Building strong relationships with stakeholders to foster project support.

Cultural and Cross-Cultural Communication

- Understanding the impact of cultural differences on project communication.
- Adapting communication styles to suit diverse project team members and stakeholders.
- Avoiding misunderstandings and misinterpretations in cross-cultural settings.

Effective communication and reporting are essential skills for project managers to ensure project success. A well-developed communication plan, regular project status reporting, and proactive engagement with stakeholders contribute to a collaborative and informed project environment. In the next chapter, we will explore the crucial aspects of project closure and the steps involved in concluding a project successfully.

Effective Project Communication Strategies

Effective project communication strategies are essential to keep all stakeholders informed, aligned, and engaged throughout the project lifecycle. Here are some key strategies to enhance project communication:

- **Develop a Comprehensive Communication Plan:** Create a well-defined communication plan that outlines the objectives, target audience, communication methods, frequency, and responsible parties for each type of communication.
- **Know Your Audience:** Understand the communication needs and preferences of different stakeholders. Tailor your communication style and approach to suit their specific requirements.
- **Use Clear and Concise Language:** Avoid jargon and technical language. Use clear and simple language to convey information effectively.
- **Regular Project Meetings:** Conduct regular project meetings to discuss progress, address concerns, and foster collaboration among team members.
- **Utilize Multiple Communication Channels:** Leverage various communication channels, such as emails, project management software, video conferencing, and in-person meetings, to reach different stakeholders effectively.
- **Active Listening:** Practice active listening during meetings and discussions. Encourage open dialogue and seek input from all team members.
- **Document Important Decisions and Actions:** Maintain clear documentation of decisions made, action items assigned, and responsibilities delegated during meetings. Share meeting minutes promptly.
- **Visual Communication Aids:** Use visual aids, such as charts, graphs, and infographics, to present complex information in a clear and easily understandable format.
- **Manage Expectations:** Set realistic expectations with stakeholders regarding project timelines, deliverables, and potential challenges. Be transparent about risks and uncertainties.
- **Provide Timely Updates:** Share project updates and progress reports regularly. Keep stakeholders informed about milestones achieved and upcoming activities.
- **Address Concerns Promptly:** Be responsive to stakeholder concerns and questions. Address issues promptly and proactively.
- **Risk Communication:** Clearly communicate project risks, their potential impact, and mitigation strategies. Engage stakeholders in risk assessment and decision-making.
- **Change Management Communication:** Effectively communicate any changes to project scope, schedule, or resources. Provide rationale and anticipated benefits of changes.
- **Celebrate Successes:** Recognize and celebrate project successes with the team and stakeholders. Acknowledge individual and collective contributions.
- **Feedback Mechanisms:** Establish feedback channels to encourage stakeholders to share their thoughts and concerns. Act on feedback and communicate the actions taken.
- **Adapt to Cultural Differences:** Be mindful of cultural differences in communication styles and adapt accordingly when working with a diverse team or international stakeholders.
- **Project Website or Portal:** Create a dedicated project website or portal where stakeholders can access project-related information, updates, and resources.
- **Positive Reinforcement:** Provide positive feedback and encouragement to team members to foster a positive and motivated working environment.

By implementing these effective project communication strategies, project managers can enhance collaboration, manage expectations, and build strong relationships with stakeholders.

Good communication is a cornerstone of successful project management, leading to improved project outcomes and stakeholder satisfaction.

Creating Progress Reports

Creating progress reports is an essential part of project management, as they provide stakeholders with an overview of the project's status, accomplishments, and potential issues. Progress reports should be clear, concise, and easy to understand. Here's a step-by-step guide to creating effective progress reports:

- **Determine Report Frequency:** Decide on the frequency of progress reports based on the project's timeline and stakeholder requirements. Common intervals include weekly, bi-weekly, or monthly reports.
- **Define Report Content:** Outline the key elements to be included in the progress report. Typical sections may include:
    - **Project Overview:** Briefly describe the project's objectives and scope.
    - **Accomplishments:** Highlight key milestones, tasks completed, and deliverables achieved since the last report.
    - **Current Status:** Provide an overview of the project's current status, including any changes or deviations from the original plan.
    - **Key Performance Indicators (KPIs):** Include relevant metrics and KPIs that measure project progress and performance.
    - **Risks and Issues:** Identify any significant risks or issues that may impact the project's success and describe mitigation efforts.
    - **Next Steps:** Outline upcoming activities, milestones, and tasks to be completed in the next reporting period.
    - **Resource Utilization:** Include a summary of resource allocation and utilization to date.
    - **Budget Status:** Present an overview of the project's financial performance, including budget spent and remaining.

- **Gather Data:** Collect accurate and up-to-date data from project team members, subject matter experts, and other relevant sources.
- **Use Visual Aids:** Incorporate charts, graphs, and tables to present data visually and make complex information more accessible.
- **Focus on Key Messages:** Keep the progress report focused on the most critical information. Avoid unnecessary details and provide a concise overview.
- **Provide Context:** Add context to the data presented by providing explanations or interpretations of the results. Help stakeholders understand the implications of the reported progress.
- **Use Consistent Formatting:** Maintain a consistent format and layout for each progress report to make it easy for stakeholders to compare information over time.
- **Proofread and Edit:** Review the progress report for accuracy, clarity, and completeness. Edit and proofread the content to ensure it is error-free.
- **Share on Time:** Submit the progress report to stakeholders according to the agreed-upon schedule. Ensure that it reaches the intended recipients in a timely manner.
- **Encourage Feedback:** Encourage stakeholders to provide feedback or ask questions about the progress report. Be open to addressing their concerns or clarifying any information.
- **Document Previous Reports:** Maintain a record of previous progress reports to track the project's historical performance and progress.
- **Continuous Improvement:** Learn from each progress report's preparation and feedback to improve future reports. Incorporate suggestions for enhancing the report's effectiveness.

By following these steps, project managers can create progress reports that effectively communicate the project's status and keep stakeholders informed and engaged. Well-crafted progress reports facilitate decision-making, help identify potential risks and opportunities, and contribute to the overall success of the project.

Conducting Project Status Meetings

Conducting project status meetings is a crucial aspect of effective project management. These meetings provide an opportunity for the project team and stakeholders to come together, discuss progress, address challenges, and align on the project's direction. Here are key steps to conduct successful project status meetings:

- **Schedule Regular Meetings:** Determine the frequency of status meetings based on the project's timeline and complexity. Weekly or bi-weekly meetings are common for most projects.
- **Set Clear Objectives:** Establish clear objectives for each status meeting. Common objectives include reviewing project progress, discussing accomplishments, identifying roadblocks, and making decisions.
- **Prepare an Agenda:** Create a well-structured agenda that outlines the topics to be discussed and the time allocated to each item. Share the agenda with participants in advance.
- **Invite Relevant Stakeholders:** Invite project team members, key stakeholders, and anyone else whose input or participation is crucial to the meeting's success.
- **Start and End on Time:** Begin the meeting promptly and ensure that it stays within the allocated time frame. Respect participants' time and keep the meeting focused.
- **Review Action Items from Previous Meetings:** Start the meeting by reviewing action items from previous meetings. Confirm completion status and address any outstanding tasks.
- **Present Project Progress:** Provide an overview of the project's progress since the last meeting. Highlight completed tasks, achieved milestones, and any changes to the project plan.
- **Address Key Performance Indicators (KPIs):** Discuss relevant KPIs and metrics that measure project performance. Analyze trends and identify areas for improvement.
- **Discuss Risks and Issues:** Identify and discuss potential risks and issues that may impact project success. Develop action plans to mitigate or resolve them.
- **Encourage Open Communication:** Create a supportive and collaborative environment where participants feel comfortable sharing their thoughts and concerns.
- **Encourage Active Participation:** Encourage active participation from all meeting attendees. Invite input from team members and stakeholders to foster engagement.
- **Use Visual Aids:** Present data and project updates using visual aids like charts, graphs, and slides. Visuals make complex information more accessible.
- **Document Meeting Minutes:** Designate someone to take meeting minutes and record key discussions, decisions, and action items. Share the minutes with participants after the meeting.
- **Follow Up on Action Items:** Ensure that action items assigned during the meeting are documented, and responsible parties are aware of their roles. Monitor progress on these tasks.
- **Stay Focused and On Track:** Keep the meeting focused on the agenda items and avoid veering off-topic. Redirect discussions if they become too detailed or irrelevant to the current agenda.
- **Summarize and End with Next Steps:** Summarize key points discussed in the meeting and identify next steps and action items. End the meeting with a clear understanding of what needs to be done moving forward.
- **Solicit Feedback:** Ask for feedback from participants on the meeting's effectiveness and how it can be improved for future sessions.

By following these steps, project managers can conduct productive and engaging project status meetings that foster effective communication, collaboration, and decision-making among project stakeholders. Regular status meetings keep the team aligned, enable early identification of potential issues, and contribute to the project's overall success.

Managing Project Documentation

Managing project documentation is crucial for maintaining organized and accessible project information throughout its lifecycle. Proper documentation ensures that project team members, stakeholders, and future project managers have access to essential records and data. Here are key strategies for managing project documentation effectively:

- **Create a Centralized Repository:** Establish a centralized and secure document management system or repository where all project-related documents can be stored, organized, and accessed by authorized team members.
- **Standardize Naming Conventions:** Implement standardized naming conventions for documents to make them easily identifiable and searchable. Include relevant information like date, version, and document type in the file names.
- **Categorize Documents:** Organize project documents into logical categories and subcategories. Common categories may include project plans, requirements, design documents, progress reports, meeting minutes, and deliverables.
- **Version Control:** Maintain version control for important documents to avoid confusion and ensure that team members are using the most up-to-date information.
- **Document Approval Process:** Establish a document approval process to ensure that all critical documents are reviewed and approved by relevant stakeholders before being finalized.
- **Document Access Control:** Control access to project documents based on roles and responsibilities. Restrict sensitive information to authorized personnel only.
- **Backup and Disaster Recovery:** Implement regular backups of project documentation to protect against data loss. Have a disaster recovery plan in place to ensure business continuity in case of unforeseen events.
- **Document Retention Policy:** Define a document retention policy to determine how long documents should be kept and when they can be archived or disposed of according to legal and organizational requirements.
- **Document Templates:** Use standardized templates for project-related documents, such as project plans, status reports, and meeting agendas, to ensure consistency and save time.
- **Metadata and Tags:** Include relevant metadata and tags for documents to provide additional context and improve searchability within the document management system.
- **Regular Document Review:** Periodically review project documentation to ensure accuracy, relevance, and completeness. Update documents as necessary based on project changes or lessons learned.
- **Collaborative Editing:** Encourage collaborative editing and document sharing among team members. Use cloud-based collaboration tools to facilitate real-time editing and feedback.
- **Document Security:** Implement security measures to protect sensitive information from unauthorized access or data breaches.
- **Train Team Members:** Provide training to project team members on the document management system and best practices for creating, storing, and retrieving documents.
- **Audit Trails:** Maintain audit trails or logs that record document access and changes made by users. This enhances accountability and transparency.

By implementing effective project documentation management strategies, project managers can ensure that project information is organized, up-to-date, and accessible to the right stakeholders. Proper documentation management contributes to better decision-making, efficient collaboration, and successful project outcomes.

Chapter 9: Project Closure & Evaluation

In this chapter, we explore the essential steps involved in effectively closing a project and conducting a comprehensive project evaluation. Project closure marks the formal end of the project's execution phase and sets the stage for the evaluation process, which helps identify successes, challenges, and opportunities for improvement.

Project Closure Process

- Defining the project closure criteria and objectives.
- Obtaining final acceptance and sign-off from stakeholders.
- Completing all outstanding tasks and deliverables.
- Conducting a final project review and documentation.

Handover and Transition

- Planning for project handover to relevant stakeholders or operational teams.
- Preparing handover documentation, training materials, and support plans.
- Ensuring a smooth transition of project deliverables to the end-users or the operational environment.

Final Financial and Resource Review

- Conducting a final financial review to ensure all expenses are accounted for and within budget.
- Reviewing resource utilization to identify areas of improvement for future projects.

Project Evaluation and Lessons Learned

- Conducting a thorough evaluation of project performance against objectives and success criteria.
- Identifying lessons learned from both successes and challenges faced during the project.
- Capturing feedback from stakeholders and team members to inform future improvements.

Celebrating Success and Recognizing Contributions

- Recognizing and celebrating project success with the project team and stakeholders.
- Acknowledging the contributions of team members and stakeholders who played a significant role in the project's success.

Documenting Project Archives

- Creating a project archive containing all relevant documents, reports, and data.
- Ensuring that the project archive is easily accessible for future reference or audits.

Project Closure Report

- Preparing a comprehensive project closure report that summarizes the entire project lifecycle, outcomes, challenges, and lessons learned.
- Presenting the closure report to relevant stakeholders and management.

Contract Closure (if applicable)

- Ensuring all contractual obligations are fulfilled and contracts are closed appropriately.
- Resolving any outstanding contractual matters with vendors or partners.

Post-Project Review and Follow-up

- Conducting a post-project review with key stakeholders to assess the project's impact on the organization and its long-term outcomes.
- Implementing recommendations and improvements identified during the project evaluation.

Project closure and evaluation are critical stages of the project management process. Proper closure ensures that all project deliverables are handed over, lessons learned are captured, and successes are celebrated. The evaluation process helps in continuous improvement and informs future project planning and execution. By effectively closing projects and conducting thorough evaluations, project managers can enhance project success rates, build institutional knowledge, and achieve greater organizational success in the long run. In the next chapter, we will explore advanced project management concepts and emerging trends in the field.

Closing Out the Project

Closing out the project is a crucial phase in project management that marks the formal conclusion of the project's execution and transitions it to the next phase or operational environment. Here's a step-by-step guide on how to effectively close out a project:

- **Confirm Project Completion:** Verify that all project deliverables and requirements have been met, and the project is ready for closure.
- **Final Acceptance and Sign-Off:** Obtain final acceptance and sign-off from key stakeholders, including the project sponsor, client, or end-users, indicating their approval of the project's outcomes.
- **Complete Outstanding Tasks:** Ensure that any outstanding tasks, activities, or open issues are addressed and resolved.
- **Handover and Transition:** Plan and execute the handover of project deliverables to relevant stakeholders or operational teams. Provide necessary training and support to ensure a smooth transition.
- **Final Financial Review:** Conduct a final review of the project's financials to ensure all expenses are accounted for and within the approved budget.
- **Resource Review:** Review resource utilization during the project to identify areas of improvement and optimize resource allocation for future projects.
- **Project Evaluation and Lessons Learned:** Conduct a comprehensive project evaluation to assess the project's performance against objectives and success criteria. Identify lessons learned from successes and challenges faced during the project.
- **Capture Feedback:** Gather feedback from project team members, stakeholders, and end-users to gain insights into the project's strengths and areas for improvement.
- **Recognize Contributions:** Celebrate project success and recognize the contributions of project team members and stakeholders who played a significant role in the project's achievements.
- **Document Project Archives:** Compile all relevant project documents, reports, and data into a project archive for future reference or audits.
- **Prepare a Project Closure Report:** Create a comprehensive project closure report that summarizes the project's entire lifecycle, outcomes, challenges, lessons learned, and recommendations for future projects. Present the closure report to relevant stakeholders and management.
- **Contract Closure (if applicable):** Ensure that all contractual obligations are fulfilled, and contracts with vendors or partners are closed appropriately.
- **Post-Project Review and Follow-Up:** Conduct a post-project review with key stakeholders to assess the project's impact on the organization and its long-term outcomes. Implement recommendations and improvements identified during the project evaluation.
- **Celebrate Success:** Organize a project closure meeting or event to celebrate the successful completion of the project and recognize the efforts of the project team.
- **Close Project Accounts:** Settle all financial accounts related to the project, including vendor payments, expenses, and reimbursements.
- **Notify Stakeholders:** Communicate the formal closure of the project to all stakeholders and relevant parties involved.
- **Update Project Documentation:** Update project documentation, such as the project charter, scope statement, and other project-related documents, to reflect the project's closure.
- **Lessons Learned Sharing:** Share the lessons learned from the project with other project managers and teams to improve future project outcomes.

By following these steps, project managers can ensure a smooth and successful closure of the project, leaving a positive impact on stakeholders and paving the way for future projects and opportunities.

Conducting Project Reviews & Evaluations

Conducting project reviews and evaluations is essential for assessing a project's performance, identifying areas for improvement, and capturing valuable lessons learned. These reviews provide valuable insights into the project's success, challenges, and overall effectiveness. Here's a step-by-step guide to conducting project reviews and evaluations:

- **Define Evaluation Objectives:** Clarify the objectives of the project review and evaluation. Determine what aspects of the project will be assessed, such as scope, schedule, budget, quality, and stakeholder satisfaction.
- **Select Evaluation Methods:** Choose appropriate evaluation methods based on the project's size, complexity, and available resources. Common evaluation methods include surveys, interviews, focus groups, and data analysis.
- **Assemble Evaluation Team:** Form an evaluation team comprising project stakeholders, subject matter experts, and individuals who were not directly involved in the project's execution to ensure an unbiased assessment.
- **Gather Project Data:** Collect relevant data and information about the project's performance, outcomes, and deliverables. Use project documents, reports, and data from various sources.
- **Assess Against Success Criteria:** Evaluate the project's performance against the success criteria and objectives defined during the project planning phase. Determine if the project achieved its intended outcomes.
- **Identify Strengths and Weaknesses:** Identify the project's strengths and successful practices that contributed to its success. Also, pinpoint weaknesses, challenges, and areas that need improvement.
- **Analyze Budget and Resource Utilization:** Review the project's financial performance and resource utilization. Assess if the project was delivered within the approved budget and if resources were used effectively.
- **Evaluate Stakeholder Satisfaction:** Gather feedback from key stakeholders, including the client, end-users, and project team members, to assess their satisfaction with the project's outcomes and overall execution.
- **Document Lessons Learned:** Capture valuable lessons learned from the project, both positive and negative. Document best practices, strategies for improvement, and recommendations for future projects.
- **Compare with Baseline Metrics:** Compare project performance with the baseline metrics established during project planning. Analyze variances and understand the reasons behind them.
- **Quantitative and Qualitative Analysis:** Use a mix of quantitative and qualitative data analysis to gain a comprehensive understanding of the project's performance and impact.
- **Identify Project Successes:** Recognize and celebrate project successes and accomplishments. Acknowledge the efforts of the project team and stakeholders.
- **Recommendations for Improvement:** Based on the evaluation findings, develop actionable recommendations and improvement strategies to enhance future project planning and execution.
- **Present Evaluation Findings:** Prepare a comprehensive evaluation report presenting the evaluation findings, lessons learned, and recommendations. Present the report to project stakeholders and management.
- **Implement Improvements:** Work with project stakeholders and team members to implement the identified improvements and lessons learned in future projects.
- **Continuous Improvement Culture:** Promote a culture of continuous improvement within the organization by integrating evaluation and lessons learned into project management practices.
- **Document Results for Future Reference:** Maintain a record of the evaluation results, findings, and recommendations for future reference and knowledge-sharing.

By conducting project reviews and evaluations, project managers can identify areas of success and improvement, enhance project outcomes, and strengthen the organization's project management practices. The insights gained from evaluations contribute to a culture of learning and continuous improvement, leading to more successful projects in the future.

Capturing Lessons Learned for Future Projects

Capturing lessons learned is a valuable practice in project management as it enables organizations to learn from past experiences and improve future project outcomes. Lessons learned are insights gained from the successes, challenges, and experiences encountered during a project. Here's a structured approach to capturing lessons learned for future projects:

- **Create a Lessons Learned Repository:** Establish a centralized repository or database to capture and store lessons learned from various projects. This repository should be easily accessible to project teams and stakeholders.
- **Identify the Right Time to Capture Lessons:** Determine the appropriate times during the project lifecycle to capture lessons learned. Common points include project milestones, major deliverable completions, and project closure.
- **Conduct Lessons Learned Sessions:** Facilitate lessons learned sessions with the project team, key stakeholders, and subject matter experts. Encourage open and honest discussions about what worked well and what could be improved.
- **Ask Specific Questions:** Ask specific questions to prompt discussions and gather relevant insights. Examples include:
    - What were the major successes achieved during the project?
    - What were the most significant challenges and how were they overcome?
    - What were the key factors that contributed to the project's success?
    - Were there any unexpected issues, and how were they addressed?
    - What could have been done differently to improve project outcomes?
- **Document Lessons Learned:** Record the lessons learned in a structured format, including the project name, date, key insights, and relevant context. Use templates or standardized forms to ensure consistency.
- **Categorize and Prioritize Lessons:** Organize the lessons learned into categories, such as project planning, risk management, communication, resource allocation, and stakeholder engagement. Prioritize lessons based on their potential impact on future projects.
- **Include Actionable Recommendations:** Provide actionable recommendations based on each lesson learned. Clearly state how these recommendations can be applied to future projects.
- **Share Lessons Learned:** Share the lessons learned with other project teams, relevant departments, and project management offices. Communicate the insights gained to promote knowledge-sharing and prevent similar mistakes in the future.
- **Implement Lessons Learned:** Ensure that the lessons learned are actively incorporated into future project planning, execution, and decision-making processes.
- **Update Project Management Processes:** Use the lessons learned to update and improve project management processes, methodologies, and best practices.
- **Encourage Continuous Improvement:** Promote a culture of continuous improvement by encouraging team members to share their experiences and insights regularly.
- **Review Past Lessons Learned:** Before starting a new project, review the lessons learned from past projects to apply relevant insights and avoid repeating mistakes.
- **Monitor and Evaluate Progress:** Regularly monitor the implementation of lessons learned in future projects. Evaluate their effectiveness and make further adjustments if needed.

By capturing and applying lessons learned from past projects, organizations can enhance their project management capabilities, minimize risks, and achieve better project outcomes. Lessons learned serve as a valuable resource for teams to build on successes, avoid pitfalls, and continuously improve their project delivery practices.

Chapter 10: Project Management Tools and Software

In this chapter, we explore the wide array of project management tools and software available to streamline project planning, execution, monitoring, and collaboration. These tools play a vital role in enhancing project efficiency, communication, and overall success. We will touch on this topic but for more in-depth knowledge and details I will leave that for our next version.

Types of Project Management Tools

- Different types of project management tools can help you become more efficient and effective but each tool needs to be analyzed for your specific situation. Some types of tools are as follows:
  - Project Planning and Scheduling Tools
  - Task and Resource Management Tools
  - Communication and Collaboration Platforms
  - Document Management Software
  - Risk Management Tools
  - Reporting and Analytics Software

Selecting the Right Tools for Your Project

- In order to choose the right project management tools you will need to base your decision on project size, complexity, team size, and budget.
- Identifying essential features and functionalities required for specific project needs is a personal requirement and should ne considered.
- Evaluating ease of use, integration capabilities, and customer support of different tools is a critical part of your analysis.

Popular Project Management Software

- Make sure to read in-depth reviews and comparisons of popular project management software, such as:
  - Microsoft Project
  - Asana
  - Trello
  - Monday.com
  - Wrike
  - Jira
  - Basecamp
  - Smartsheet
  - Teamwork
  - ClickUp
  - Notion
  - and others

Project Management Software Implementation

- Make sure you research and create best practices for introducing project management tools to a team or organization.
- How to best conduct training and onboarding team members to effectively use the selected software.
- Planning to overcome resistance to change and encouraging adoption of new tools.

Integrating Project Management Tools

- Explore the benefits of integrating project management tools with other software, such as CRM, accounting, and communication tools.
- Discussing common integration challenges and strategies to overcome them before choosing the products.

Collaboration and Communication Platforms

- Make sure to read in-depth reviews and comparisons of popular collaboration and communication platforms, such as:
    - Slack
    - Microsoft Teams
    - Google Workspace
    - Zoom
    - Microsoft SharePoint
    - and others

Mobile Project Management Apps

- Reviewing mobile project management apps that enable remote project management and real-time collaboration on the go can be extremely effective but should be considered when deciding if it is necessary for your project/Project Team.

Project Management Tool Security

- Ensure you analyze reviews and feedback regarding data security and privacy when using project management tools.
- Understanding best practices for protecting sensitive project information is critical especially when working with confidential data.

Trends in Project Management Software

- Explore emerging trends in project management tools, including AI-powered analytics, automation, and virtual collaboration.
-

Project management tools and software have become indispensable assets for modern project managers, enabling them to optimize project workflows, enhance team collaboration, and achieve better project outcomes. By selecting the right tools, integrating them effectively, and staying abreast of the latest trends, project managers can position themselves for continued success in an ever-evolving project management landscape.

Introduction to Project Management Tools

Project Management tools are software applications and platforms designed to assist project managers and teams in planning, executing, monitoring, and controlling projects more effectively. These tools play a crucial role in improving project efficiency, collaboration, communication, and overall success. They provide a centralized and structured approach to managing projects, enabling teams to stay organized, meet deadlines, and deliver high-quality results.

In the past, project management relied heavily on manual processes, spreadsheets, and paper-based documentation. However, the advent of technology has revolutionized project management, offering a wide range of tools and software to automate various project-related tasks and streamline workflows.

The key benefits of project management tools include:

- **Enhanced Planning and Scheduling:** Project management tools offer robust planning and scheduling features, enabling project managers to create detailed project plans, set milestones, allocate resources, and define dependencies.
- **Collaboration and Communication:** These tools facilitate seamless collaboration among team members, stakeholders, and clients. They provide shared workspaces, real-time communication channels, and document sharing capabilities.
- **Task and Time Management:** Project management tools allow teams to track tasks, assign responsibilities, set deadlines, and monitor progress. They also help in tracking project timelines and resource utilization.
- **Reporting and Analytics:** These tools generate comprehensive reports and dashboards, providing valuable insights into project performance, risks, and key performance indicators (KPIs).
- **Document Management:** Project management tools offer document storage and version control features, ensuring that all project-related documents are centralized and accessible to authorized users.
- **Risk Management:** Many tools include risk management functionalities, enabling project managers to identify, assess, and mitigate potential risks throughout the project lifecycle.
- **Integration Capabilities:** Project management tools often integrate with other software applications, such as accounting, customer relationship management (CRM), and communication platforms, facilitating seamless data exchange and improving overall workflow efficiency.
- **Mobility and Remote Collaboration:** With the rise of mobile project management apps, teams can collaborate and access project information from anywhere, enhancing remote work capabilities.

Different project management tools cater to diverse project requirements, team sizes, and industries. Some tools are designed for specific project methodologies, such as Agile or Waterfall, while others offer versatility to accommodate various project management approaches.

Popular Project Management Software

There are numerous project management software options available in the market, each offering unique features and functionalities to cater to diverse project needs. Here are some of the popular project management software widely used by teams and organizations:

- **Microsoft Project:** Microsoft Project is a comprehensive project management tool that provides robust planning, scheduling, and resource management capabilities. It offers Gantt charts, task tracking, and reporting features, making it suitable for both small and large projects.
- **Asana:** Asana is a user-friendly project management tool that emphasizes task organization and collaboration. It offers a visual interface, project timelines, and integrations with other popular apps.
- **Trello:** Trello is a flexible and visual project management tool that uses boards, lists, and cards to organize tasks and projects. It is ideal for smaller projects and agile teams.
- **Monday.com:** Monday.com is a versatile work operating system that allows teams to plan, track, and collaborate on projects using customizable boards and automation.
- **Wrike:** Wrike is a cloud-based project management software with features like task management, time tracking, document sharing, and real-time collaboration.
- **Jira:** Jira is widely used in software development and IT projects. It offers issue tracking, agile project management, and integration with development tools like GitHub.
- **Basecamp:** Basecamp is a simple and user-friendly project management tool with to-do lists, file sharing, and messaging, suitable for small to medium-sized projects.
- **Smartsheet:** Smartsheet is a collaborative work management platform that combines spreadsheet-like functionality with project management features.
- **Teamwork:** Teamwork is a project management and team collaboration platform with task management, time tracking, and integration capabilities.
- **ClickUp:** ClickUp is a customizable project management software with features like task management, goal tracking, and time tracking, suitable for various industries.
- **Notion:** Notion is an all-in-one workspace that allows teams to create databases, wikis, and documents for project organization and knowledge sharing.
- **Zoho Projects:** Zoho Projects is a cloud-based project management tool with features like task management, time tracking, and issue tracking.
- **Airtable:** Airtable is a flexible collaboration platform that combines the ease of use of a spreadsheet with project management features.
- **Podio:** Podio is a customizable project management and collaboration platform that allows teams to build their own workspaces and workflows.

When selecting a project management software, consider factors such as the size and complexity of your projects, the needs and preferences of your team, integration possibilities, and your budget. Many tools offer free trials, which can help you assess their suitability for your specific project management requirements.

Utilizing Technology for Efficient Project Management

Utilizing technology is essential for efficient project management in today's fast-paced and interconnected world. Project management software and digital tools offer a wide range of benefits that streamline processes, improve collaboration, and enhance project outcomes. Here are some ways to leverage technology for efficient project management:

- **Project Planning and Scheduling:** Use project management tools to create detailed project plans, set milestones, and define task dependencies. Gantt charts and timeline views help visualize project schedules and identify critical paths.
- **Task and Resource Management:** Digital tools facilitate task assignment, progress tracking, and resource allocation. Team members can update task statuses in real-time, promoting accountability and transparency.
- **Collaboration and Communication:** Leverage communication platforms and collaboration tools to facilitate seamless interaction among team members, stakeholders, and clients. Instant messaging, video conferencing, and shared workspaces promote effective teamwork.
- **Document Management:** Centralize project documents and files in cloud-based document management systems. This ensures easy access, version control, and document sharing, reducing the risk of information silos.
- **Risk Management:** Use risk management software to identify, assess, and mitigate project risks. Data analysis and modeling tools can help anticipate potential challenges and devise contingency plans.
- **Time Tracking and Reporting:** Implement time tracking tools to monitor project hours, resource utilization, and task progress. Generate automated reports to keep stakeholders informed about project status.
- **Mobile Project Management Apps:** Embrace mobile apps that enable remote project management and on-the-go collaboration. Mobile access keeps teams connected and informed, regardless of their location.
- **Integration Capabilities:** Integrate project management tools with other business systems, such as CRM, accounting, and HR software. Seamless data exchange streamlines workflows and avoids duplication of effort.
- **Automating Repetitive Tasks:** Utilize automation tools to streamline repetitive tasks, such as email notifications, updates, and task assignments. Automation improves efficiency and reduces manual errors.
- **Real-time Data and Analytics:** Utilize analytics and data visualization tools to gain insights into project performance, identify trends, and make data-driven decisions.
- **Virtual Collaboration:** Leverage virtual collaboration tools, augmented reality, and virtual reality to facilitate remote collaboration, especially in distributed teams.
- **AI and Machine Learning:** Explore AI-powered project management tools that can predict project outcomes, analyze risks, and optimize resource allocation based on historical data.
- **Continuous Improvement:** Implement feedback mechanisms and post-project reviews to continuously improve project management practices based on lessons learned.

By leveraging technology, project managers can optimize project processes, enhance communication, reduce manual effort, and ultimately increase project success rates. However, it's essential to strike a balance between technology and human judgment, ensuring that the technology supports and enhances project management practices rather than replacing critical decision-making skills and human interaction.

Chapter 11: Agile Project Management

In this chapter, we delve into the principles, methodologies, and practices of Agile Project Management. Agile is a dynamic and iterative approach that emphasizes flexibility, collaboration, and customer-centricity. It has gained popularity in various industries for its ability to adapt to changing requirements and deliver value incrementally.

Understanding Agile Principles

- Explaining the Agile Manifesto and its core values: individuals and interactions, working solutions, customer collaboration, and responding to change.
- Discussing the importance of embracing change and maintaining a focus on delivering business value.

Agile Methodologies

- Introducing various Agile methodologies, including:
    - Scrum
    - Kanban
    - Extreme Programming (XP)
    - Lean Agile
    - Dynamic Systems Development Method (DSDM)
    - Feature-Driven Development (FDD)
    - Crystal
    - Agile Unified Process (AUP)

Agile Project Lifecycle

- Exploring the iterative and incremental nature of Agile project lifecycles.
- Describing how Agile projects progress through planning, executing, and reviewing iterations or sprints.

Scrum Framework

- In-depth examination of the Scrum framework, including roles (Product Owner, Scrum Master, Development Team), events (Sprint Planning, Daily Stand-ups, Sprint Review, Sprint Retrospective), and artifacts (Product Backlog, Sprint Backlog, Increment).

Implementing Agile in Organizations

- Addressing challenges and best practices for introducing Agile methodologies in traditional organizations.
- Discussing the importance of cultural transformation, team empowerment, and executive buy-in.

Scaling Agile for Large Projects

- Strategies for scaling Agile to manage large, complex projects with multiple teams and dependencies.
- Introduction to scaling frameworks like SAFe (Scaled Agile Framework) and LESS (Large-Scale Scrum).

Agile Project Estimation and Planning

- Discussing Agile estimation techniques, such as Planning Poker and Story Points.
- Exploring Agile planning practices, including Backlog Refinement and Release Planning.

Agile Project Metrics and Reporting

- Identifying key metrics and indicators used to measure project progress and team performance in Agile projects.
- Discussing Agile reporting practices for stakeholders' visibility and decision-making.

Agile Project Risk Management

- Adapting risk management practices to the iterative nature of Agile projects.
- Discussing how Agile encourages early risk identification and mitigation.

Advantages and Limitations of Agile Project Management

- Analyzing the benefits of Agile, including improved customer satisfaction, adaptability, and team morale.
- Addressing the challenges and limitations of Agile, such as potential resistance to change and scope management.

Agile Project Management offers a flexible and customer-focused approach to project delivery. By embracing Agile principles, methodologies, and practices, project managers can foster collaboration, increase responsiveness to change, and deliver value in a rapidly evolving business environment. Whether implementing Agile for the first time or refining existing practices, understanding the core concepts of Agile is fundamental to achieving project success and meeting customer needs. In the final chapter, we will provide a comprehensive summary of this book and offer key takeaways for effective project management in diverse industries and project scenarios.

Understanding Agile Principles & Methodologies

Agile is a set of values and principles that guide project management practices, focusing on iterative and incremental development, flexibility, collaboration, and customer-centricity. Agile methodologies are the practical frameworks and approaches that implement these principles. Let's explore Agile principles and some of the popular Agile methodologies:

Agile Principles:

- **Customer Collaboration over Contract Negotiation:** Engage customers and stakeholders throughout the project to gather feedback, prioritize requirements, and deliver solutions that meet their evolving needs.
- **Responding to Change over Following a Plan:** Embrace change as a natural part of the project lifecycle. Be adaptable and open to modifying plans to accommodate new information and requirements.
- **Delivering Working Solutions over Comprehensive Documentation:** Prioritize delivering functional and valuable solutions over extensive documentation. While documentation is essential, Agile focuses on producing tangible results.
- **Individuals and Interactions over Processes and Tools:** Value people and effective communication within the team. Collaboration and teamwork are emphasized over relying solely on processes and tools.

Agile Methodologies:

- **Scrum:** Scrum is one of the most popular Agile methodologies. It divides work into fixed-length iterations called "sprints," usually lasting two to four weeks. The team holds regular meetings, including Sprint Planning, Daily Stand-ups, Sprint Review, and Sprint Retrospective.
- **Kanban:** Kanban is a flow-based Agile methodology. It visualizes work on a Kanban board, with tasks moving through stages. It provides real-time visibility into work status and promotes a steady flow of work.
- **Extreme Programming (XP):** XP emphasizes technical practices to ensure software quality. It includes practices such as pair programming, test-driven development (TDD), continuous integration, and frequent releases.
- **Lean Agile:** Lean Agile combines Agile principles with Lean thinking to optimize processes and eliminate waste. It focuses on delivering value to the customer quickly.
- **Dynamic Systems Development Method (DSDM):** DSDM is an Agile framework that prioritizes on-time delivery and meeting business needs. It emphasizes incremental development, collaboration, and user involvement.
- **Feature-Driven Development (FDD):** FDD is an iterative and incremental Agile methodology that focuses on building features and delivering small working increments.
- **Crystal:** Crystal methodology is a family of methodologies that adapts Agile principles based on the specific project's characteristics, team size, and criticality.
- **Agile Unified Process (AUP):** AUP combines Agile practices with the Rational Unified Process (RUP) framework to provide a more flexible and iterative approach.

Agile methodologies empower teams to deliver high-quality solutions efficiently by fostering frequent communication, continuous improvement, and customer involvement. Each methodology offers unique benefits, and the choice of the right approach depends on the project's nature, team composition, and organizational culture.

Agile is particularly well-suited for projects with evolving requirements, uncertain environments, and where customer feedback is critical. By embracing Agile principles and methodologies, project managers can enhance project success rates and adapt to the ever-changing demands of the business landscape.

Scrum, Kanban & Other Agile Frameworks

Scrum, Kanban, and other Agile frameworks are popular methodologies that implement Agile principles and practices to manage projects. Each framework has its unique approach to project management, emphasizing different aspects of flexibility, collaboration, and iterative development. Let's explore Scrum, Kanban, and a few other Agile frameworks:

- **Scrum:** Scrum is a widely used Agile framework that divides work into fixed-length iterations called "sprints." Each sprint typically lasts two to four weeks, during which the development team works on a set of prioritized features from the product backlog. Key roles in Scrum include:
    - **Product Owner:** Represents the stakeholders, defines the product backlog, and sets priorities.
    - **Scrum Master:** Facilitates the Scrum process, removes impediments, and ensures the team adheres to Scrum practices.
    - **Development Team:** Cross-functional team responsible for delivering working increments of the product at the end of each sprint.

Scrum ceremonies include Sprint Planning, Daily Stand-ups, Sprint Review, and Sprint Retrospective. The Scrum framework provides a structured and iterative approach to product development.

- **Kanban:** Kanban is an Agile framework that focuses on continuous delivery and visualizing work on a Kanban board. The board consists of columns that represent different stages of work, such as "To Do," "In Progress," and "Done." Tasks or user stories move through these columns as they progress.

Key principles of Kanban include limiting work in progress (WIP), continuously improving processes, and responding to bottlenecks. Kanban is especially suited for workflows with variable demand and no fixed iterations.

- **Extreme Programming (XP):** Extreme Programming (XP) is an Agile framework that emphasizes technical excellence and software quality. XP practices include:
    - Pair Programming: Two developers work together at one workstation, continuously reviewing each other's code.
    - Test-Driven Development (TDD): Developers write tests before writing code to ensure code correctness and maintainability.
    - Continuous Integration: Developers frequently integrate their code into a shared repository, triggering automated builds and tests.

XP aims to improve code quality, reduce defects, and support fast, continuous delivery.

- **Lean Agile:** Lean Agile combines Agile principles with Lean thinking, aiming to eliminate waste and optimize value delivery. It focuses on identifying and delivering the most valuable features first, minimizing delays, and ensuring a smooth flow of work.
- **Dynamic Systems Development Method (DSDM):** DSDM is an Agile framework that prioritizes on-time delivery and meeting business needs. It provides a framework for scaling Agile to large projects and teams.
- **Feature-Driven Development (FDD):** FDD is an iterative and incremental Agile methodology that focuses on building features and delivering working increments.
- **Crystal:** Crystal methodology is a family of methodologies that adapt Agile principles based on the specific project's characteristics, team size, and criticality.

Each Agile framework has its strengths and is suitable for different project scenarios. Project managers can choose the most appropriate Agile framework based on the project's requirements, team dynamics, and organizational culture to maximize project success and customer satisfaction.

Implementing Agile Practices in Your Projects

Implementing Agile practices in your projects requires careful planning, stakeholder buy-in, and a willingness to embrace change. Here are some steps to effectively introduce Agile practices into your projects:

- **Understand Agile Principles and Methodologies:** Ensure you have a clear understanding of Agile principles and methodologies. Familiarize yourself with frameworks like Scrum, Kanban, or Lean Agile to determine which one aligns best with your project and team.
- **Start with a Pilot Project:** Consider starting with a small pilot project to test Agile practices before fully adopting them across all projects. This allows you to learn and adjust without risking larger projects.
- **Build a Cross-functional Agile Team:** Assemble a cross-functional team with diverse skills and expertise to work collaboratively and effectively. The team should include members representing all necessary disciplines to deliver the project.
- **Define Clear Roles and Responsibilities:** Clearly define roles and responsibilities for team members, including the Product Owner, Scrum Master (if using Scrum), and Development Team. Ensure everyone understands their roles and how they contribute to the project's success.
- **Create a Product Backlog:** For Scrum projects, create a product backlog containing all the features, tasks, and requirements for the project. Prioritize items based on their value and complexity.
- **Conduct Sprint Planning:** If following Scrum, conduct Sprint Planning meetings to select items from the product backlog for the upcoming sprint. Set achievable sprint goals and establish a sprint duration (usually two to four weeks).
- **Hold Daily Stand-up Meetings:** Conduct daily stand-up meetings to promote communication and collaboration within the team. Each team member shares progress, challenges, and plans for the day.
- **Implement Visual Project Management:** Use visual tools like Kanban boards or task boards to represent work items and their status. This provides transparency and helps the team stay organized.
- **Encourage Continuous Improvement:** Foster a culture of continuous improvement within the team. Regularly conduct Sprint Retrospectives (for Scrum) or Kaizen meetings to discuss what went well, what could be improved, and take action on areas for enhancement.
- **Facilitate Customer Involvement:** Involve customers and stakeholders throughout the project to gather feedback, validate requirements, and ensure the delivered product meets their needs.
- **Monitor Progress and Adapt:** Regularly review project progress and adjust plans as needed. Agile projects are flexible and embrace change, so be prepared to adapt to evolving requirements.
- **Provide Training and Support:** Ensure team members are adequately trained in Agile practices and provide ongoing support to address any challenges that arise during the transition.
- **Celebrate Successes:** Recognize and celebrate achievements and successes within the team. Positive reinforcement boosts team morale and motivation.
- **Share Learnings Across the Organization:** Document and share the learnings from implementing Agile practices, both successes and lessons learned, to promote knowledge-sharing and continuous improvement across the organization.

Implementing Agile practices requires a shift in mindset and collaboration among team members. It is essential to have a supportive organizational culture that encourages experimentation, learning, and continuous improvement for successful adoption of Agile in your projects.

Chapter 12: Real-world Project Management Examples

In this chapter, we will explore real-world project management examples from various industries and domains. These examples highlight how project management principles and methodologies are applied to address unique challenges, achieve project objectives, and deliver successful outcomes. By examining these case studies, readers can gain insights into practical project management practices and strategies that have been proven effective in different scenarios.

Real-world project management examples provide valuable insights into how project managers navigate challenges, apply methodologies, and lead teams to success. By examining diverse case studies from different industries, readers can gain practical knowledge and inspiration to apply effective project management practices in their own projects. Remember that each project is unique, and adaptability, collaboration, and continuous improvement are essential for achieving successful outcomes in a dynamic and ever-changing business environment.

Real Case Studies of Successful Project Management

Case Study 1: A Large Waterway Canal Expansion Project

Project: Expansion of the Canal to accommodate larger vessels and increase capacity.

Success Factors:

- Comprehensive project planning and risk analysis to address geological challenges and potential cost overruns.
- Collaboration between international engineering firms, government agencies, and local stakeholders.
- Implementation of a state-of-the-art locks system to handle larger ships and increase efficiency.
- Effective project management to complete the expansion within the projected timeframe and budget.

Case Study 2: New State of The Art Aircraft Project

Project: Development and production of a new state of the art aircraft.

Success Factors:

- Agile project management practices to adapt to design changes and evolving market demands.
- Collaboration between international teams and suppliers to manage the global supply chain.
- Utilization of advanced composite materials to reduce weight and increase fuel efficiency.
- Successful certification and delivery of the aircraft to various airlines worldwide.

Case Study 3: The High-Speed Rail Expansion Project in Japan

Project: Construction of a critical high-speed rail network in Japan.

Success Factors:

- Comprehensive project planning and engineering studies to optimize routes and ensure safety.
- Strong government support and public-private partnerships for funding and execution.
- Use of innovative technologies and construction methods to minimize disruption to the environment and existing infrastructure.
- Timely completion and operation of the railway network, revolutionizing transportation in Japan.

Case Study 4: The Olympic Games

Project: Organizing and hosting the Olympics in a very large European City.

Success Factors:

- Detailed project planning and coordination with multiple stakeholders, including international sports organizations and government agencies.
- Extensive infrastructure development and venue preparation to host various events.
- Effective security measures to ensure the safety of athletes and spectators.
- Successful execution of the games, receiving praise for organization and hospitality.

Case Study 5: A Major Space Telescope Repair Mission

Project: Repair and upgrade the premier space telescope.

Success Factors:

- Precise project planning and simulations to ensure the success of the delicate spacewalks.
- Collaboration between NASA, international space agencies, and astronaut teams.
- Innovative engineering solutions to fix the telescope's optical problems and extend its operational life.
- Successful completion of multiple servicing missions, significantly enhancing the telescope's capabilities.

These real case studies demonstrate how effective project management practices, such as meticulous planning, collaboration, risk management, and innovative problem-solving, have led to successful outcomes in diverse and complex projects. The ability to adapt to challenges, leverage the expertise of stakeholders, and maintain a focus on delivering quality results are critical factors in achieving project success.

Learning From Project Failures & Challenges

Learning from project failures and challenges is crucial for improving project management practices and preventing similar issues in the future. Project failures can be caused by various factors, including inadequate planning, poor communication, scope creep, lack of stakeholder engagement, and unexpected risks. Here's how project managers can learn from failures and challenges:

- **Conduct Post-Project Reviews:** Hold comprehensive post-project reviews or retrospectives to analyze what went wrong and what could be improved. Encourage open and honest discussions to identify root causes and gather insights from team members and stakeholders.
- **Identify Lessons Learned:** Document lessons learned from both successful and failed projects. Create a repository of best practices, challenges encountered, and strategies for overcoming difficulties. This knowledge-sharing helps future projects benefit from past experiences.
- **Analyze Project Data:** Analyze project performance data, such as budget overruns, missed deadlines, and scope changes. Identify patterns and trends to uncover recurring issues that need to be addressed.
- **Encourage Feedback from Team Members:** Create a culture of feedback and learning within the team. Encourage team members to share their observations and suggest improvements regularly.
- **Review Change Management Processes:** Evaluate change management procedures to ensure that changes are adequately assessed, documented, and communicated. Address scope creep and its impact on project success.
- **Improve Risk Management:** Revisit risk management practices and enhance risk identification and mitigation strategies. Ensure that risks are regularly assessed, and contingency plans are in place.
- **Enhance Communication and Stakeholder Engagement:** Assess communication practices within the team and with stakeholders. Strengthen communication channels to ensure everyone is informed and aligned with project goals.
- **Invest in Training and Skill Development:** Provide training and skill development opportunities for project managers and team members. Equip them with the necessary tools and knowledge to handle project complexities effectively.
- **Adapt Project Management Methodologies:** Consider adapting project management methodologies to better suit the project's unique characteristics and challenges. Agile methods may be more suitable for projects with evolving requirements.
- **Set Realistic Expectations:** Ensure that project objectives, timelines, and deliverables are realistic and achievable. Avoid setting unrealistic expectations that can lead to disappointment and project failure.
- **Seek External Consultation:** In challenging situations, consider seeking advice from external consultants or subject matter experts. Their fresh perspective can offer valuable insights and solutions.
- **Monitor and Measure Progress:** Implement robust project monitoring and tracking mechanisms to detect issues early. Regularly measure project performance against predefined metrics and KPIs.

By learning from failures and challenges, project managers can continuously improve their project management practices and enhance project success rates. A proactive approach to addressing problems and fostering a culture of continuous improvement leads to more efficient and successful project outcomes.

Adapting Best Practices for Your Projects

Adapting best practices for your projects is essential to enhance project efficiency, effectiveness, and success. Best practices are proven methods and approaches that have been successful in similar projects or industries. Here's how you can adapt best practices to suit your specific project needs:

- **Conduct a Project Assessment:** Start by conducting a thorough assessment of your project's requirements, objectives, constraints, and stakeholders. This analysis will help you identify which best practices are most relevant and applicable to your project.
- **Research Best Practices:** Research and study best practices in project management literature, industry-specific resources, and case studies. Look for practices that align with your project's goals and can address potential challenges.
- **Tailor Practices to Your Project:** Adapt best practices to suit the unique characteristics of your project. Consider factors such as project size, complexity, timeline, and team composition. Customize the practices to fit your project's specific needs.
- **Engage Stakeholders:** Involve key stakeholders, including team members and clients, in the process of adapting best practices. Seek their input and feedback to ensure that the chosen practices are feasible and aligned with their expectations.
- **Implement Agile Principles:** Embrace Agile principles such as flexibility, collaboration, and customer-centricity to adapt best practices iteratively. Agile allows you to continuously improve and adjust practices based on real-time feedback and changing project dynamics.
- **Encourage Knowledge Sharing:** Promote knowledge-sharing among team members to share insights and experiences from past projects. Encourage open communication and learning from both successes and failures.
- **Measure Performance:** Establish performance metrics and key performance indicators (KPIs) to measure the effectiveness of adapted best practices. Regularly review performance data to identify areas for improvement.
- **Create a Best Practices Repository:** Develop a centralized repository of adapted best practices, lessons learned, and success stories. This repository can serve as a valuable resource for future projects and team members.
- **Seek Expert Guidance:** Consult with project management experts or experienced professionals to get advice on adapting best practices. External insights can provide valuable perspectives and innovative solutions.
- **Be Open to Iteration:** Be prepared to iterate and refine adapted best practices as the project progresses. Stay open to feedback and be willing to make adjustments as needed.
- **Document and Review:** Document the adapted best practices and ensure they are shared and communicated across the team. Regularly review and update the practices as the project evolves.
- **Celebrate Successes:** Acknowledge and celebrate successes resulting from the implementation of adapted best practices. Positive reinforcement encourages the team to continue applying effective strategies.

Adapting best practices requires a proactive and adaptive approach to project management. By incorporating proven methods while tailoring them to your project's unique requirements, you can optimize project outcomes and achieve greater project success.

Congratulations! You've completed The Ultimate Project Management Handbook. With the knowledge gained from this book, you are well-prepared to tackle various projects successfully. Remember, project management is an evolving field, so keep learning, adapting, and refining your skills. Always be open to new challenges and opportunities for growth. Happy managing!

www.ingramcontent.com/pod-product-compliance
Lightning Source LLC
Chambersburg PA
CBHW051532240526
45471CB00019B/958